Gail M. Ragen

GLASS HOUSES:
RAISING KIDS WITH MY EX

Gail M. Ragen is an attorney, wife and mother of three grown children. She is also an ex-wife and co-parenting partner with the father of her children. For years, while raising children cooperatively with her ex, Gail wanted to share her families' experience in raising three children in two households. Because the story features her children, Gail waited until they were adults and could consent to being included in this book. All three children enthusiastically support its publication. Gail also asked for and received the full support of her ex-husband in sharing the following story of how they transitioned from mismatched partners in a broken marriage to cooperative parents and friends.

GLASS HOUSES:

Raising Kids With My Ex

GAIL M. RAGEN

NOTE TO READERS

This publication contains the opinions and ideas of its author. It is intended to provide helpful and informative material on the subject matter covered. It is sold with the understanding that the author and publisher are not rendering legal, medical, health or any other kind of personal professional services in this publication. The reader should consult his or her attorney, medical, health or other competent professional before adopting any of the suggestions or ideas in this book or drawing any inferences from them. The author and publisher expressly disclaim any liability, loss or risk, personal or otherwise, which is incurred as a consequence, directly or indirectly, of the use and application of any of the contents of this book.

Scripture taken from *THE MESSAGE*. Copyright © 1993, 1994, 1995, 1996, 2000, 2001, 2002. Used by permission of NavPress Publishing Group.

ISBN: 0989071901
ISBN 13: 9780989071901

GLASS HOUSES:

Raising Kids With My Ex

DEDICATION

To my mother, with love

❡INTRODUCTION

When I was a child, my parents built a modern glass house on Mercer Island, Washington, overlooking Lake Washington and the Olympic Mountains. I lived in the glass house with my parents, my two older sisters and my baby brother. I loved to wander the gardens, following my brother as he learned to walk, or to play near my mom and dad, who were great gardeners and seemed the picture of happiness while planting maple and fir trees, rhododendrons and ferns. But when I was ten, our glass house shattered. My parents divorced, and I lost not only the home I loved, but also my sense of stability and, in a very real sense, the notion of who I was.

When my parents divorced, Washington, like most states, required "grounds" for divorce, which meant the spouse filing for divorce had to prove that he or she was innocent and that the other spouse (the "guilty" one) had engaged in severe and specific wrongdoing. Despite the passage of nearly fifty years since my parents' divorce, I still shudder when I hear the words mental cruelty and abandonment—painful reminders of the legal and emotional struggles between my parents when they were splitting. Fault divorce has since been abolished by all fifty states out of recognition that courts have neither the resources nor the ability to sort through marital complexities and breakdowns. The assignment of blame did little more than temporarily assuage the feelings of one spouse while publicly vilifying the other. And the innocent children not only bore the brunt of the enhanced anger within the family, they also suffered society's judgments and reprimands.

Once, my best friend's grandmother casually suggested in my presence that someone did not meet her high standards because he or she came from a "broken home." I believed the sting of her comment was aimed at me, and I felt the heat of shame because I came from a divorced family. My shame was tinged with anger because I knew I had done nothing to deserve punishment. I was a good person, a kind girl doing well in school. This self-righteous woman vented her scorn on an innocent child. Everyone in my family, it seemed, had to wear scarlet letters. We were *all* divorced.

Years later, when my husband, Peter, and I divorced, fault divorce had long since been abolished in California, so we had no state-sponsored cruelty to contend with. And divorce had become more socially acceptable over the years. But I still worried that my children would feel the pain I had experienced when my parents divorced. Peter, on the other hand, had never had a divorce in his family. He, too, was afraid of harm coming to our children, or of losing them in a battle with me. I did not want to feel bitter toward Peter or carry a grudge for the rest of my life. I wanted to be happy and to raise happy, confident children. I believe Peter felt the same way.

In the final weeks of our marriage, when we were on the brink of separating, a tragedy in Peter's office—a mass shooting—rocked us to our cores. Peter narrowly escaped being murdered. This traumatic event, which took the lives of friends and colleagues, drove home to us the fragility of life and the importance of seeking peace instead of revenge. Having been spared tragedy, we did not want to squander our lives bickering with each other and making our families miserable. Spurred by our own backgrounds and grateful that we had full lives ahead of us, Peter and I decided to make our divorce work for ourselves and, especially, for our three young children.

Making peace during and after our divorce was not easy. We had a long history of arguing with one another over issues large and small. By the time we reached the end of our marriage, we had stopped communicating, and we both harbored a great deal of anger and hurt. As much as I wanted to get along with Peter on an intellectual level, I was unsure how to get there emotionally. How could we achieve peace in divorce when we had so thoroughly failed to accomplish peace during our marriage? When discussing this challenge with my sister, she reminded me of one of Mahatma Gandhi's many pearls of wisdom: "Be the change you seek." That sounded like a good idea, but I wasn't sure how to apply such a concept to my life. The only thing I knew for sure was that, even though my marriage to Peter had failed, we would be co-parenting our children for many years to come. Our daughter was a toddler and our two sons were in elementary school. We had hundreds, if not thousands, of school and sporting events to attend in upcoming years—not to mention college decisions to make, weddings to plan, and grandchildren to share in the more distant future. Peter and I could divorce each other, but we were still inextricably linked through the daily lives of our children.

As a child of divorce, I knew that the way Peter and I treated each other during and after our divorce would impact our children's happiness and sense of well-being for the rest of their lives. I also realized that our children would unconsciously adopt parenting styles based in part on how they were parented. Knowing how my actions would shape our children and have ripple effects into future generations, I wanted to be the best parent I could be. And despite the adversity of divorce, I realized I had the opportunity and responsibility to behave well as a co-parent and to cooperate with Peter, even when our emotions ran high.

The senseless killing of Peter's colleagues, one of whom was a young father, forced me to reckon with mortality and to question more deeply what kind of person I wanted to be and what kind of legacy I wanted to leave behind for my children and grandchildren. In the aftermath of the murders, Peter and I spoke more kindly to each other than we had in a long time. We acknowledged our good fortune in having narrowly escaped catastrophe, and we pledged to cooperate with each other during and after our divorce. We agreed not to say critical things or to badmouth each other, which at first required a bit of acting. Of course, we stumbled into minefields and stepped on each other's toes during and after our divorce. But when tempted to fall back into old patterns of arguing, we tried to resist those knee-jerk reactions and reminded ourselves that we were committed to peace for our children. Over time, as we cultivated our inner voices of reason, there was less acting required, and we found that we had created a rich peace dividend for ourselves, as well as for our children. As Peter and I cooperated and treated each other with courtesy, the anger and hurt ebbed away and was replaced by mutual respect, improved communication and a shared commitment to cooperatively raise the children we brought to this earth.

Because of this mutual commitment to harmony, Peter and I knew we could calmly interact with one another, exchange the children with pleasantries, and rest assured that neither was undermining or back-stabbing the other. And by leaving our long history of anger and resentment behind, Peter and I both became happier people, opening up space in our hearts to find love with others downstream.

Peter and I are both remarried now. His wife, Ellen, has a charming and talented teenage son. She also has two doctoral degrees and is fluent in five languages. She's a great mom and step-mom. I am married to Jim, a man with whom I have found the intimacy and validation I had so long yearned for. Jim has two grown children who have enriched my life. Peter and I and our spouses share an extended family—all four of our mothers are alive and in their late eighties. We all occasionally socialize together, especially during the holidays (which can be so difficult and painful for divorced families).

People used to say I was lucky to have a great relationship with my ex. Yes, I was lucky that Peter wanted to cooperate as much as I did. Successful parenting by exes requires mutual effort. While one ex can take the lead, cooperation is ultimately a two-way street. Fortunately, Peter and I were starting in a better space than some couples, in that we did not have an abusive relationship or pose any danger to ourselves, each other, or our children. We had simply unraveled over time into a dysfunctional married couple.

Like most divorcing couples, by the time we actually split, our marriage was broken beyond recovery, and no amount of counseling, wishing or pretending could change that. After years of an unhappy marriage, we did not simply wake up one day and find ourselves in a happy divorce. Rather, we picked ourselves up from the rubble of our broken marriage and decided to get along after our divorce. The peace we created for ourselves and our children in the aftermath of divorce was not a condition that descended upon us, nor was it conferred or negotiated through the legal system. Rather, Peter and I forged peace through conscious cooperation and compromises strung together day-to-day over fifteen years after our divorce. This effort required us both to grow up, slow down, and put our resentments and petty differences aside. We made the effort and our efforts paid off. When we remarried, our partners admired and supported our efforts to positively parent our children post-divorce, and we did the same for them in return. And today, all these years later, we may not be a typical family, but we are a happy and peaceful one.

Not long ago I saw a friend of mine, a divorce lawyer I hadn't seen in a long time. We got to talking and, when she asked, I told her that the kids were doing well and that Peter and I were still working together successfully. She shook her head and told me she'd like to require all of her clients to take a course—before she represented them—on getting along. "How did you do it?" she asked. "You should write a book!"

How did we do it? I wondered.

I asked my husband, Jim, "What do people see? Why are Peter and I different from so many other divorced parents?"

He thought for awhile and said, "Because you and Peter are divorced, people know you've suffered anger and disappointment with each other. But when they see you interact, they see courtesy and cooperation, not rudeness or antagonism. You're kind toward each other, not bitter. And people see the results in your three lovely children."

Peter and I have now been divorced for eighteen years, and for the most part our co-parenting is over. Our two sons, Peter Jr. and Ben, are in their mid-twenties and making their way in the world. (In the family we still call Peter Jr. by his childhood nickname, "PJ," and to avoid confusion, I do so here.) PJ is earnest, fun-loving and hard-working. Ben is pursuing his degree in business after working several years for talent managers in Hollywood. They are both engaging young men who fill their parents with pride. Our third and youngest child, Leigh, is now in college. Leigh was a toddler when we divorced and is now twenty years old. She is happy, confident, a great student, and deeply loved by her older brothers and the parents and step-parents who raised her in two households.

We have reached the end of an era for our family, now that our kids are launched. Jim and I have moved to the California desert. Peter lives with Ellen and her son, Alexander, in Seattle. Peter and I have seen each other less often as our children have become adults, but we still communicate on a frequent basis—usually in brief e-mails about our children. We still get together for the holidays from time to time. Most importantly, we will always have the satisfaction of knowing we succeeded in raising our children together after our marriage ended. As our child-rearing days draw to a close, I feel our family was and is a success. Despite the inevitable pain of divorce, Peter and I learned to rein in our tempers in difficult times, to reject the blame game, and to move on with our separate but still intertwined lives. Ultimately, we found love with new partners and widened the circle of our extended family. Over time, old wounds and scars healed or simply faded away.

Every once in awhile, I'm asked, "Why didn't you two stay married? If you could get along so well after divorcing, surely you could have worked things out." I have also received some criticism for suggesting that divorce can be an acceptable solution to an unhappy marriage. Along this line, I once received a not-so-nice comment from an editor who wrote, "Divorce IS a disaster and the narrator needs to acknowledge this." Yes, divorce *can* be a disaster, as can marriage. Neither one nor the other is inherently good or evil. But divorce, while disruptive, need not be a disaster. Outsiders who insist that this is always the case display the negative societal judgments that divorced families can and must reject.

As to the former, more positive comments, Peter and I tried long and hard—as most divorced couples do—to work out our problems and stay married. But for all kinds of reasons, some of which I include here, we couldn't pull it off. For us, like so many others, divorce was the better choice. Given that we were divorcing, we owed it to our children to behave courteously and kindly to each other and our children—even when it was challenging to do so. Now, as I reflect on the past and anticipate the future, I am profoundly grateful to Peter and to our current spouses that we committed ourselves to a real and lasting peace.

☙1

During the year leading up to my divorce, I was traveling frequently for business. On a trip through Chicago, a colleague treated me to dinner. Over our meal, I told him I was going through a divorce. My colleague said he was sorry to hear it and, as I shared some of my regrets about the past and fears about my future, he gave me this sage advice:

"Learn from the past and plan for the future, but live in the present." He smiled as I nodded and mulled this over. "In other words," he continued, "don't dwell on the past or dread what lies before you. Sure, you have some challenging days ahead, but keep your priorities straight and you'll land on your feet. You always do."

All these years later, I still recall my colleague's advice because he helped me recognize that I should not get bogged down in recriminations over past disappointments or cringe in fear of my unknown future. To this day, when going through challenging times, as we all do, I try to bring some wisdom from past experiences, and tamp down my fears about the future so that I can thrive in the present. Of course, I've made mistakes in my past and will make more in the future. But as George Eliot once wrote, "It is never too late to be what you might have been."

When Peter and I divorced, memories of my own parents' divorce flooded through my mind. To a large extent, my desire and commitment to get along with Peter was fueled by my memory of the pain I had endured as a child when my parents divorced. That pain carried over into my adult life, and I did not want my own children to carry the scars caused by chronic parental conflict.

The most difficult thing I experienced when my parents split up was feeling torn emotionally between two people I loved and needed. When parents involve their children in fights during a divorce (or within a marriage), the children often feel forced to take sides. The trauma accompanying such torn loyalties can cause deep psychological scars. Something organic is lost that can never be replaced. That void can be filled with anger, resentment, and insecurities that ripple out through generations. My parents "buried the hatchet" many years ago, and even though my father is now limited by Alzheimer's disease, both of them have encouraged me to share my story in the hope that other parents going through divorce can minimize its impact on their children and head off potential social, emotional and psychological problems.

❧❧

In the early years of their marriage, my parents were a popular couple with an active social life. My dad was one of four athletic brothers and had been a star football player in college. My mom had been a top student, published poet, and football cheerleader in college. Like so many others in their generation, my parents helped fuel the baby boom after World War II. They married young and went on to have four children: Linde, Alice, Gail (me) and Bob. We kids were spread out in age over fourteen years.

My mother was a bit of a princess and did not worship my father in the way he initially idolized her. In their early years, Dad held her on a pedestal—and she believed she belonged there. But she was stable, honest and predictable. One always knew exactly where one stood with my mother, who to this very day is disinclined to mask her emotional state. My father, on the other hand, had a Jekyll and Hyde personality. The Dr. Jekyll in him was a talented, well-read, thoughtful and funny man, and a loving father. His Mr. Hyde persona was cruel, self-indulgent, egotistical and unapologetic. I'll always struggle to reconcile my father's dark side with the cheerful, loving, funny, and sweet man he could be. You just never knew from moment to moment which Dad you would get.

❧❧❧

In the years before their divorce my parents fought from time to time, but I never had any inkling that they would split apart one day. To the contrary, I felt safe within my family and had an innate sense of coming from and belonging to both of my parents. In happy times, my parents would tell me and my siblings about the days we were born. They told us they'd rushed to the hospital in a freak November snowstorm when Linde was born; they were twenty-two years old and had been married for ten months. Linde was a whirlwind of activity and kept everyone running, my mom would say. Alice came two years later and was round-faced, sweet and contented. I was born four years later on Saint Patrick's Day. "You had beautiful ringlets that I loved to brush," my mother would say. When I was nearly eight years old, a baby boy joined our brood. I still recall my parents rushing home from a game of bridge the evening before my sister Alice's twelfth birthday. My mother's water had broken and my parents, flushed with excitement, were on their way to the hospital.

"Please wait until tomorrow!" Alice wailed as they rushed out the door. "I want a baby for my birthday!"

"I'll try," my mother called back over her shoulder. "But no guarantees!"

Alice got her birthday wish. Our brother, Bobby, was born just after midnight. When Bobby came home from the hospital with our parents a few days later, the whole family gathered around him.

"He has blue eyes!" we girls exclaimed.

We all had brown hair and eyes like Mom, although our faces were shaped more like Dad's. Our little brother was a blue-eyed blond like our dad, but my mother said his face was shaped like hers. We laughed and admired our blue-eyed boy. My sisters and I counted fingers and toes, searching for resemblances and differences between ourselves and "our" new baby. Our family was together and filled with joy. I believed it would always be that way. But that was not to be.

Three years after that joyful day, my father told my sisters he had a girlfriend in another city and was planning to divorce

Mom in about a year. He told them not to tell her. Of course, Linde and Alice could not carry the burden of such a secret. Shaken and frightened, they went to our mother with the terrible news. My mother reacted with shock, anger and dismay. She confronted my father, who admitted his plan, and all hell broke loose in our household. My mother kicked Dad out of the house, and their marriage exploded into fragments.

After learning from her daughters that Dad was leaving, my mother slammed the door behind Dad with crushing force. The windows rattled and shook in our glass house. A chill gripped my heart as I watched my family fall apart.

My parents joined in battle, and I overheard some ferocious arguments. I was desperate to know what was going on. I surreptitiously eavesdropped on one particularly nasty phone call.

"How dare you tell my children the things you did," my mom said, her voice shaking with fury.

"They're my kids, too, and I can tell them whatever I want," Dad retorted.

"I will get a court order to prevent you from talking to them that way."

"Well, then, I will fight you for *custody*."

"Ha! Good luck!" My mother slammed the receiver down in the telephone cradle, ending that verbal brawl. I quickly hung up the extension in my parents' bedroom, reeling from the things I'd heard. I thought court was a place criminals went on their way to jail. And I had never heard the word custody. All I knew was that my parents were fighting over us kids. My world had turned upside down overnight and I had no idea what to do.

❧❧

While my parents' divorce headed toward court, my mom took me and Bobby to an appointment with her lawyer. I sat with Bobby in the gloomy waiting room of the lawyer's office, feeling a bone-weary exhaustion. After the appointment, we rode home together in silence. My mom was lost in her own painful thoughts, and when we got home she locked herself in her bedroom. She started smoking and dropped weight. My mother was devastated, and for several days I hovered outside her bedroom door, playing with my little brother. Even at his tender age, Bobby knew something was dreadfully wrong. I did my best to entertain him, but I was frightened for my mother, my siblings and myself.

After a few days, my mother emerged from her solitude and stood crestfallen and shell-shocked in the kitchen. I didn't know what to say.

"Your father is leaving me," Mom said. She sagged against the kitchen counter and wept. Her pain was palpable. "He is leaving us."

I, of course, had no answers and was utterly helpless. I went to my mom and wrapped my arms around her slender frame. "I love you," I said. "And I will always stay with you." I felt the weight of the world on my shoulders. My mother hugged me back. I knew our family would never be the same. My childhood was essentially over because I had to grow up and be strong.

Thus we began our new and altered life. My mom rallied for days at a time after my father was gone, but then spiraled down into sadness and anger again. She could not mention my dad without gritting her teeth and slinging arrows. I did not see my father at all for weeks. My feeling of safety and security had been largely stripped away. I felt like a baby bird that had fallen from its nest long before it had developed wings to fly.

My sisters were older and spent more time with their friends—away from home. Alice spent a lot of time with my Dad, which crushed my mom. I was sad, and lost interest in playing with my neighborhood friends. Their moms and dads were together. They enjoyed family picnics and vacations while my parents went separate ways. It hurt to see everything I was missing. I tried to help my mother as much as I could, mostly by playing with and babysitting my little brother while Mom gathered herself and tried to rebuild her life.

During this time, I sometimes felt the urge to upstage my parents and to let everyone know how hard this was on me. "How do you think *I* feel?" I wanted to say when my mom or dad complained to me. But a tiny voice inside told me to bear up and shut down all such feelings. There was no room for any more discord in the family. I stuffed my own needs and fears deep in the pit of my stomach where they festered with no outlet.

Statistics show that children of divorce tend to marry young, and that is what happened in my family. Linde married first, at the age of seventeen; she never lived at home after the divorce. Alice went out of state to college soon after Linde left home. That left my mother and my brother and me to form a new type of nuclear family.

My mother felt the fall from grace that accompanies divorce, and so did I. The social stigma surrounding divorce still exists, but was far more pronounced in the sixties. My mom's social circle shrank because divorcées held lower social status than married women. My mother was accustomed to being held in high esteem, and she keenly felt the shame. I also felt a shift in my social world. I knew that we now were "different." My friends all knew my parents were getting divorced. Some felt sorry for me, and I didn't like that. I had always been a leader among my peers—someone they admired—and I did not relish feeling diminished. How I wished I could be a happy and carefree kid again.

❧2

My parents ultimately settled without going to court, and my mom was given primary custody. Under their agreement, my father received "reasonable visitation rights," but there was no set schedule, so my parents wrangled over the visits. In the first year or so after my parents split, I did not spend much time with my father. I had no say in the timing or frequency of the visits, which bore no relationship to my own social activities. I had to go on visits whether I wanted to or not, and I felt like a shuttlecock. The inconvenience, though, paled in comparison to being torn emotionally between my parents. They both wanted support that was trying and exhausting to give. From my perspective, every ounce of support given to one parent was an ounce taken from the other. I felt terribly guilty and was caught in a vicious cycle.

For several years, Mom and Dad barely spoke to one another. They often told us to convey messages from one to the other. Their anger sometimes spilled over onto us, the messengers, and their facial expressions and nonverbal cues also telegraphed negativity toward one another. My ensuing feelings of confusion, disloyalty, shame and fear added pounds of grief to my already heavy heart.

Once, when I was visiting my dad after the divorce, he complained to me that he had been treated unfairly by the judge and that people drove to the courthouse from miles around just to read his divorce papers. I felt more shame, humiliation and sadness. I was too young to know what divorce papers were, but I pictured faceless people hunched over their steering wheels, streaming through the rain-soaked roads to the courthouse (wherever that was) to pore over our family business.

Like most divorced families, our financial status deteriorated when my parents split up into two households (my mother in a house with us kids, and my dad in an apartment). The post-divorce budget required the sale of our beautiful glass house. Along with the house went the surrounding neighborhood. I had been well liked, happy and carefree in that neighborhood. I'd belonged. All of this came to a stop when my parents divorced and we sold our house and moved.

Despite my mother's anger, sadness and humiliation over becoming divorced and losing our home, she righted the listing ship of our now smaller household. Over time, she gained her emotional footing and made our new home pretty and comfortable. (I got my love of home decorating from her.) Even though she sometimes suffered from depression, she remained a wonderful cook. And Mom and I did have fun together, in spite of the difficult times. Our life had been seriously disrupted and altered, but it wasn't a disaster. The summer after my parents divorced, two of my sixth-grade classmates died—one from leukemia, the other from a boating accident. Those *were* disasters. Divorce is never fun, but most everyone can and does survive.

Friends and family can be a great source of support for divorcing families, even though it is often difficult for them to know what to do. My grandparents on both sides of the family behaved exceptionally well during and after the divorce. Their stability was one silver lining in the crisis. My mother's parents lived nearby and provided her with an invisible safety net. Most importantly, they never breathed a word of discord to our recovering family. They must have been furious with my father for leaving, but they never threw fuel on the fire. My father's mother had been widowed for years, but she also lived nearby, and she was always kind and loving. She helped Dad cover his alimony and child support when cash was running low. She made "cowboy stew" and delicious ginger cookies whenever we visited her, and she enjoyed showing us pictures of all our East Coast aunts, uncles and cousins.

We visited with our West Coast relatives frequently, but gathering with our East Coast relatives was a rare and special treat. Importantly, our large extended family—grandparents, aunts, uncles, and cousins on both coasts—helped provide a sense of normalcy, and reminded me that I had far-reaching familial roots, even though my parents were divorced.

§♥♥§

I learned as a child of divorce how keenly children feel their parents' pain. As my mother gained her bearings, my emotional state was closely linked to hers. For the most part, when my mom was happy, I was happy. If she wasn't, I was stressed out or sad. But I continued to suppress my emotions, especially willing myself never to cry. Something told me that if I ever started crying, I would never be able to stop, and I would break into a million pieces.

I also suppressed my fears, of which I had many. With my father gone, my mother and I had lost our "protector," and at night if we heard a scary noise we had no choice but to investigate on our own. One night after we'd gone to bed, I thought I heard something downstairs. I slipped into my mother's room and gently shook her.

"Mom," I whispered in her ear, "I think I heard something."

"What? Where? What?" my Mom rose up on an elbow as she woke from a deep sleep.

"Downstairs, I think. Something woke me up."

"Oh no. It's probably just the house creaking. Just a minute. Here I come."

Mom and I crept arm-in-arm to the top of the stairway and began tiptoeing down. My heart was pounding, and I felt Mom's trembling arm. We'd made it halfway down the staircase when we heard a popping sound and stopped. We looked at each other with wide eyes, then screamed at the top of our lungs. We sprinted back up the stairs, our knees practically grazing our chins, and when we reached the top of the stairs, we burst out laughing at how ridiculous we'd looked. My mom was in a pink shortie nightgown and could have been devoured by the boogeyman in one bite. I would have made a light dessert.

"You should have seen the look on your face when we screamed," I said, bending over and clutching my sides with laughter.

"Well, you looked pretty ridiculous yourself!" Mom said.

When we stopped giggling, no monster had appeared and we'd lost our investigative steam. "If anyone was down there, we probably scared them away with those screams," I said. Anyway, we couldn't face the dark, so I climbed into bed with my mom and brother. Mom and I snuggled together in her double bed, with Bobby tucked between us, and we hoped for the best.

∞∞∞

Weeks would go by between visits with my dad—but I gradually started seeing him more. My mom hated me to go, and I missed her and my friends when I was gone. I was bored during those early visits. Dad tried to entertain me by reading with me or showing me how to load the dishwasher or make an apple pie. I think he wanted to connect with me better and was trying to find a way. He knew I was horse-crazy and that my aunt had taught me to ride. I'd long dreamed of having my own horse. One day when I was visiting my dad, he told me he knew of an Arabian horse for sale and asked if I wanted to go see it.

"Yes!" I answered. I was a die-hard horse lover, and had a particular attraction to Arabian horses, which are known for their beauty, intelligence and endurance. My dad and I drove to the property, where a farmhand pointed out a tall chestnut horse among the herd. Dad had never handled a horse in his life, so I went out to catch him. Sytan, as the horse was named, was beautiful.

My dad helped me saddle Sytan and then said, "I'd better ride him first."

Dad was a natural athlete, and one of his great—or exasperating—qualities was that he thought he could do anything (and he usually could). So he calmly took the reins in one hand, placed his foot in the stirrup, and began to swing himself onto the saddle. Sytan took off at a dead run toward the watching herd. I stood paralyzed as Dad's leg flailed over the horse's back. He rolled over Sytan's side, hit the ground, and somersaulted in the dirt before coming to a stop. Before I could move or think, Dad got up and started brushing himself off. Sytan rejoined the herd, prancing with his head high.

My dad walked back to me and said, "Well, do you want to try him?"

"Yes," I said. I hoped I could do better than he had.

As Dad dusted off, he gave me some advice that proved valuable many years later when I had to bail off a running horse. It also helped teach me to be brave before taking a fall. He said, "If you need to get off when he's running, let your legs roll under him and tuck into a ball before you hit the ground so you don't break your neck. That's the best way to do it."

I caught Sytan, rode him without falling off, and fell in love. Sytan became my soul mate. He was a handful, but I rode him everywhere. I made new friends with other kids on the island who rode horses. Sytan was instrumental in my belief that, despite the breakup of my family and all the pain it caused, I could still have great times and lots of freedom. To his credit, my dad later told me that he used to lie awake in bed at night worrying that he had been reckless to buy me such a wild horse. But he thought I had the courage and skill to control Sytan. And he was right.

Buying and supporting my horse was one of many good things my father did for me when he was on good behavior. But his dark side kept popping up. When I was sixteen, my father started looking at me differently, and he began talking to me in explicit detail about his sexual exploits with a twenty-year-old woman. I didn't want to hear about it, but I didn't know what to say or how to make him stop. This became a pattern. He also frequently criticized my mother behind her back.

"Women lose their sex appeal when they turn thirty," he often said. "After that men lose interest in them." My mother was then forty years old and beautiful, but she was apparently too old for my father. He was pursuing college-age women. What did that mean for my own future? It was all devastating and overwhelming.

In between his sexually graphic tales, my father interspersed talk of Shakespeare, literature and mathematics, along with long discourses about his childhood. I enjoyed his talk of literature and math, but his graphic sexual talk and increasing references to my sexual attractiveness made me ill. Neither my mother nor anyone else could do anything to stop him.

❦

Dealing with my father's demons became a lifelong challenge, and there is no doubt that I was better off as an adolescent not living under the same roof with him. But, despite the challenges, like most children of divorce, I survived—and in many ways, thrived. I excelled in school and enjoyed close friendships. Although I had boyfriends, I avoided sex—as well as alcohol and drugs. I was mature for my age. But below the surface, I struggled with self-esteem problems. When I looked in the mirror, I did not see the slender, attractive young woman I was. I began dieting and obsessing over my weight. By the time I turned sixteen, I'd developed bulimia, an eating disorder that I went to great lengths to hide from everyone in my life. I wanted control over my body—control over my life.

When I was seventeen, my sister Alice married a young man who had just graduated from the United States Air Force Academy. Many of their college friends converged upon my mother's home for the wedding. One of them was a handsome young man I'll call Rob. While I was sitting among my sister's college-age bridesmaids, Rob mistook me for a college girl. There I sat, suntanned, with waist-length hair and a body slimmed by nerves and bulimia: he fell in love at first sight with who he thought I was. I was star struck by the cadets and the dashing drama of the full-dress, crossed-swords wedding. Rob, who had just graduated from the Academy, was five years older than I, but we were matched as a couple for the wedding ceremony. Rob was dressed in full military whites and I wore a soft pink, silk bridesmaid's dress.

"You look beautiful," he said as we waited our turn to walk down the aisle together. "Marry me. Let's get married right now—make it a double wedding."

I smiled and briefly envisioned myself as a bride next to Alice in this fairy-tale wedding. As Rob and I lined up to take our turn down the aisle, I whispered back, "I just finished my junior year in high school, not college!"

Rob was taken aback by my age, but he continued his pursuit long after my sister's wedding, insisting we should be married. I was amused, flattered and swept off my feet. I fantasized about how cool it would be to have fine china like Alice's, not to mention an apartment. And, oh yeah, a husband! Ultimately, Rob persuaded me that we should be together. I hastened my graduation from high school by doubling my coursework and started college in Boulder, Colorado, while my high school friends went to the prom and finished their senior year. I didn't mind missing the prom and my graduation walk—I was eager and ready to start my adult life. I joined a sorority, made new friends, and sped through two years of college while carrying on a long-distance relationship with Rob.

At nineteen, I married Rob. Having barely dated anyone else, I was extremely inexperienced—not to mention young, stressed, repressed and unprepared for marriage. To his credit, Rob was loving and patient. But the more I kept him at bay sexually, the more frustrated and demanding he became, and the more guilt-ridden and turned-off I felt. As it turned out, I wasn't so mature after all.

Rob and I moved quite a bit while he was in the Air Force, so the rest of my college education was a bit of a patchwork; but I completed my bachelor's degree with excellent grades. When Rob finished his service, he started graduate school in San Antonio, Texas. Soon after, I was accepted to law school at the University of Texas in Austin. For the first time in my life, I sensed that I would soon possess the education and means to support myself. That heady feeling was accompanied by an overpowering desire for personal freedom. I did not want to be married anymore. I divorced Rob after only five years of marriage, hurting him in the process. Unfortunately, as time would prove, I lacked the maturity and self-awareness to stop myself from jumping from the frying pan into the fire.

❦3

I met Peter in May 1977 when we were both law students at the University of Texas in Austin. Peter and I were assigned to the same small section, where I first noticed him among my new classmates. Peter had an angular, handsome face and dark hair to his shoulders. He seemed to radiate intellectual intensity. On our first day of law classes, our section leader asked everyone to briefly describe his or her background. When his turn came, Peter said he'd graduated from UT Austin's Plan II (the university's honors program) and then gone to graduate school at Harvard, where he'd completed everything except his dissertation for a PhD. He said he'd spent the past two years studying languages and playing trombone in jazz bands in France and Germany.

When it came my turn to speak, I said I had been wrapping gift packages at a department store since graduating from the University of Texas. I meant to poke a little fun at myself, as I often did when I felt insecure, but it was true: I had been wrapping gift packages while Peter and many other classmates pursued their advanced degrees. Although I was impressed by my peers' academic accomplishments, I was proud of myself for getting into this competitive class based purely on my academic performance. I quickly made many friends, loved law school and believed I was in my niche.

The first time Peter and I spoke to each other, we were sitting at an outdoor lunch table among a group of law students. He and I had a brief argument over some obscure legal doctrine we were studying. I was unaccustomed to arguing with people over anything, let alone obscure legal doctrines. I thought, "I'd better get used to arguing, because I plan to be a litigator." Still, I thought Peter was a bit much, and I studied and socialized with a mellower group of friends. Later in the year, I bumped into Peter on campus and he invited me to go to a jazz club that same evening. (What? I thought we were oil and water!)

"You're probably just feeling badly about arguing with me so aggressively the first time we met," I said with a laugh.

"I don't remember any argument," he said. "I'm asking you out because you're great looking."

I accepted Peter's invitation, and as we drove to the jazz club, he told me he'd played trombone for years. He was friends with the members of Passenger, one of Austin's hottest bands. I had never heard jazz fusion and was intrigued by this new world of musical improvisation. The lead sax player, Paul, was a close friend of Peter's, and he visited with us during the band's break. I liked him a great deal. I could not then know that he would become a lifelong friend and the godfather of my second son. After we left the club, Peter and I went dancing at an outdoor club called Liberty Lunch, where more of his friends were playing Cumbia music. Again, we hung out with the musicians and danced to the energetic Latin beat. After that first date, we began seeing each other in earnest— eating, dancing, and studying together in the library in the evenings.

✂✷✂

"I'm babysitting my three-year-old godson this afternoon," Peter said one day as we were walking out of class into the hot Austin sunshine. "I'm taking him to swim at Barton Springs. Do you want to hang out with us?" I hadn't been around little kids for awhile, but I thought it was quaint and cool for a twenty-eight-year-old guy to be willing to babysit.

"Sure," I said. "That'd be fun." Soon after we arrived at Peter's house, his friend Alan arrived on the doorstep holding the hand of an adorable little boy with blond hair and big brown eyes. Alan was laid back and friendly. He had a heavy Texas accent that I found charming. I was impressed by Peter's easy and close friendship with his childhood friend. (I had long since lost touch with almost all of my own childhood friends.) Peter seemed more relaxed than usual, and his Texas accent deepened when he talked with Alan.

"Do you want to go swimming, Matteo?" Peter asked, picking the little boy up and tossing him in the air. I soon learned that Peter called close friends by goofy, made-up nicknames. Alan was "Nernst" to Peter. And Matthew clearly loved being called Matteo, the Spanish version of his name.

"Yes! Let's go!" Matthew/Matteo answered. I could tell from the little boy's instant excitement that he and Peter had done this before. Peter and I trundled Matteo into the car and drove to Barton Springs Pool, Austin's famous, spring-fed swimming hole. We spent the afternoon there, and Peter was great with his little godson. He never talked down to Matteo. He had lots of fun and laughed with him, all the while watching the little boy carefully as he played in the water.

Seeing Peter with Matteo reminded me how much I had loved to spend time with my brother, Bob, when he was a little boy. I'd often taken him to swim at a park at Lake Washington. I'd wave and smile as Bobby jumped into the water making funny faces and big splashes. Matteo also made me think of children in general and how wonderful they are. I was twenty-four and far from any thoughts of motherhood. But I looked at Peter and thought, "He will make a great dad." Little did I know as we lounged on the grassy banks of Barton Springs that I would marry Peter and have three kids with him.

❡4

As I spent more time with Peter, I learned that he talked on the phone with his parents a lot. Peter was an only child. His parents still lived in a small town west of Fort Worth, where Peter had grown up.

"How are Gretchen and Bob?" Peter would ask. "How is Aunt Edith?" Peter always wanted to know how his aunts and uncles and friends back home were doing. He was concerned when family or friends were sick or had problems. I could tell from the beginning that Peter had strong family ties and values.

Peter and I were attracted to each other intellectually and—at least briefly—sexually. Although we were spending almost all of our time together, I found him mysterious and unreachable. We were polar opposites in so many ways. When we first looked at our law school class pictures, we cracked up. Peter's looked like a mug shot of Charles Manson, and I resembled Polly Purebred in my round-necked sweater.

"You look like a total hippie," I informed him.

Peter laughed and said, "I just ducked out of the pouring rain into a photo booth. I didn't know they were going to use this picture as my class photo."

"Well, there it is," I said with a grin.

"Look at you," he said, pointing to my photograph. "You look like a sexy sorority girl."

"That's right," I said. "I am."

"Who would ever dream that we would be together?" he asked as we compared photos.

"But opposites attract, right?"

Although we laughed about our differences when we were law students, we had no idea how wide the gap between us was and would later become. I had spent the previous five years living on or near military bases with my first husband while Peter, who is four years older than I, had been in the doctoral program at Harvard, and then lived in Europe. We did not yet know that our differences were no laughing matter.

It turned out that our first meeting at the lunch table was just a warm-up match in a zero-sum game. Peter and I had emotional, raise-the-roof arguments from the outset of our relationship. I hated to argue, but we pushed each other's buttons and were determined to "go to the mat" to prove a point. We latched onto our own positions as if the world depended upon them. Peter was a skillful arguer, and he was well stocked with facts to back up his positions. Even when I could see he made a valid point, I felt he was bullying me, and I wouldn't concede. I could not seem to overcome my defensive reactions. I would become entrenched in my argument and wasn't mature or enlightened enough to recognize my own foolish pride. Neither, apparently, was Peter. We were a hot-headed pair. Once, when we were driving in my car on the freeway, we broke into an argument over a foreign policy issue. Our emotions and voices rose, and Peter lost his temper, smashing his fist into the windshield. To our mutual shock, the glass shattered into a million pieces and crumbled into our laps. I screamed and drove to the nearest freeway exit with the wind buffeting my face and the tattered edges of my former windshield flapping wildly.

"I am so sorry," Peter wailed into the wind. "I didn't mean to break it!"

"You smashed out my windshield!" I shrieked.

"I'm so sorry. I'll pay to have it replaced." Peter put his face in his hands and apologized profusely. He was never violent toward *me*, and he'd been shocked when the windshield exploded under his fist. But we couldn't seem to curb our tirades. Peter would sometimes close his eyes with frustration and smash his fist into a pillow or the air. I found it all very stressful, but I was not about to concede my rock-solid positions. We argued about everything under the sun. When we made up after a fight, Peter would half joke, half moan, "How can such a dainty woman be such a tough fighter?" (Maybe my stubbornness was genetic. My mom's father affectionately called my grandmother Concreta.) Naturally, I thought our disagreements were Peter's fault—after all, I didn't argue with anyone else.

We also had good times together. In between classes, studying and working, we canoed Texas rivers, played poker with friends, partied in New Orleans, visited each other's families, and began to plan a life together. Peter loved to see me happy and, in our last semester of law school, helped me pay for and support a beautiful Arabian horse.

Shortly after I moved in with Peter during law school, he told me that his attraction to me was no longer as high as it had first been. Of course, I was hurt and concerned, but on a deeper level I was relieved to be free of pressure. My first marriage had ended largely because I couldn't handle the constant sexual demands. And my father's inappropriate talk about sex hadn't helped me at all. "I want you to be sexually free!" my father would often say. But all of his talk about sex inhibited rather than liberated me. By the time I became involved with Peter, my sexual drives were stirring and I wanted closeness and intimacy. But Peter and I marched to different drummers, and we never achieved true, intimate satisfaction with each other. There was always something missing. We should have known better, but we both overlooked the fundamental flaws in our relationship.

Peter and I did not know that our lack of intimacy would grow into a gaping hole at the heart of our relationship and marriage. We couldn't and didn't talk about this void of intimacy, probably because we knew it would be the death knell of our relationship. As a result, the emotional distance between us gradually grew until it became a chasm we could not bridge.

¶5

When we met, Peter had traveled a great deal overseas. For years, while Peter was young, his father had led Southern debutantes on tours through Europe. This was in the days before many American college women traveled to Europe on their own. So although Peter grew up in a small town, he'd spent his summers traveling with gorgeous young women and staying in fancy places like the Ritz Carlton in Paris. He passionately loved to travel and had written about much of Eastern Europe for Harvard's *Let's Go Europe* travel guide.

I had never vacationed in Europe, or even Mexico, until Peter and I got together. My only experience traveling out of the United States was living for six months with Rob near a remote air force base in Korea. I'd worked as a switchboard operator on the base, which was located in a dark forest near the bottom of Pork Chop Hill. One night while taking a short-cut to work through the pitch-black forest, I was chased down a steep path by a rifle-toting soldier. He'd mistaken me for an intruder—and I'd mistaken him for a monster. I left Korea after six months, telling Rob I wanted to go home. After saying goodbye to Rob at the Seoul airport (he accompanied me as far as the authorities permitted), I found myself in a pushing, shoving sea of Koreans. I was bewildered, frightened, unable to understand the language and unwilling to push into the crowd toward the gate. Fortunately, a tall, young American woman with bright red hair was also in the airport throng. She saw my plight and came to my rescue.

"You just have to push!" she explained, placing a friendly hand on my back and propelling me forward. She shepherded me through the frightening process.

Years later, I was still hesitant to travel outside the country; I told Peter I wanted to try western European destinations to get warmed up. But Peter was tired of those places and wanted to explore developing countries. We traveled to Haiti and to Mexico while we were in law school. I found the poverty of Haiti oppressive and frightening, and I was nearly drowned in a parasailing mishap behind a speedboat in Mexico. After those experiences, I had no hankering to explore any more developing countries.

Peter not only loved to travel the world, he wanted to know and visit with people from other countries. He'd been treated generously in France when he studied French at the Sorbonne and in Berlin where he had studied German. He wanted me to be open to having foreign visitors stay with us. I viewed all of this with trepidation; I'm an introvert and crave privacy in my home. We had knock-down, drag-out fights about traveling. He told me he wanted to take his children around the world someday. Fine, I thought. Whatever.

Later I learned to lighten up, and I made ten trips to Europe in as many years. Two of our closest friends were French, and I have never been more elegantly entertained than in their gorgeous home near Calais, France. But for me, traveling overseas was a learning process.

⪧⪦

In one of my favorite movies, *Cool Hand Luke*, a prison warden, after whacking Paul Newman over the head with a whip and shoving him into a ditch, says: "What we've got here is a *failure to communicate.*" Paul Newman repeats the line to the warden in a later scene that must be seen to be appreciated. In any event, the line has become a classic because almost everyone on earth has experienced a problem—often a big one—that can be attributed to a failure to communicate.

Before Peter and I married, we had the good sense to discuss whether we wanted children. We agreed that each of us did, in fact, wish to have children someday. To be more precise, he wanted at least one child and I wanted at least two or three. To establish this much, we had one of our fiery arguments over the merits and drawbacks of having an only child (which he had enjoyed being) versus having several, which I thought was better. We had this debate in my car and, at one point (to protect my new windshield), I ordered him out of the car. I spun gravel as I left him standing on the side of the road. We were in a remote mountain area at the time, so I came back for him after a few minutes. He was standing on the side of the road with his hands in his pockets. We dropped the subject of children and did not discuss it again, let alone reach a mutual agreement of any sort, before we tied the knot.

Our failure to communicate was a terrible mistake because we had fundamentally different views of how we would raise our child or children. I just *assumed* that I would be the one to stay at home and raise them. That's what my mother had done. That's what his mother had done. As far as I was concerned, that was a given. Sure, I might continue to work for awhile as a lawyer, but my true role and purpose in life would be as a wife and mother. I never asked Peter if he shared the same assumption. And as it turned out, he most assuredly did not expect or want me to leave my law job and stay home to raise our children.

Peter, for his part, did not ask me if I was prepared to practice law indefinitely after having children. He had assumed that because we met in law school we would both practice law, even after we became parents. He assumed and intended that the daily, hands-on childcare would be provided by babysitters or nannies. Not only did we fail to unearth this fundamental misunderstanding before we married, we never discussed it during the five years we were married before having children. I believed that, as a mother, I would be the best person—the natural person—to raise the children day-to-day. Peter simply did not see things that way. He did not think that would be fair to him. This failure to communicate set us up for more profound disagreement and disappointment than anything we had previously experienced and was, for years, a ticking time bomb in our marriage.

6

Peter and I married immediately after we graduated from law school. We had both been hired by law firms in San Francisco, and we found a charming Pacific Heights apartment in a Victorian building across from Lafayette Park. The building was a bit "long in the tooth," but it had some nice features, like a lovely lobby with large, checkered black-and-white tiles. Our apartment was on the top floor and had a great view of the city. We reached our fourth-floor apartment by using an old-fashioned elevator with an interior metal gate. The elevator groaned, clanged and banged, announcing the comings and goings of everyone in the twelve-unit building.

We loved living in San Francisco. From the beginning, though, our work was extremely demanding. Peter had worked in high-intensity law offices before and during law school, and he better anticipated how demanding the practice of law would be in San Francisco.

"We'll have to work insane hours and deal with some really difficult personalities," he told me. He also said, "We need to give each other permission in advance to quit on the spot if anyone is ever abusive to us."

I readily agreed, but I didn't fully appreciate the demands of big-firm practice until I began working. I was a litigator, and Peter practiced in the area of health care. I worked seven days a week for over a year. I enjoyed it for the most part, despite the steep learning curve and grueling hours. I had a nine-month antitrust trial out of town in my third year of practice. Peter also worked crushing hours and became extremely active in health policy issues. That old saying, "The law is a jealous mistress," is an understatement. The law can be a merciless taskmaster, and it is no surprise that attorneys have high rates of depression and divorce.

Our marriage had a rocky start. After we moved into our San Francisco apartment, we both began studying for the California Bar Examination. Of course, we were both nervous about taking the California Bar, which had less than a 50 percent pass rate at the time. One evening as we read our preparation materials, Peter looked at me and said, "One of us is likely to fail."

I looked at him like he was insane. "That is just crazy," I said. "Neither one of us has ever failed an exam."

"But the pass rate is under 50 percent and there are two of us. So there is a good chance that one of us will fail."

Instantly, I became fighting mad. It was hard enough to study for the Bar without having my confidence undermined. And *who* did Peter think was going to fail? Me? I could not imagine him thinking he would fail. If that were his concern, why not say he was worried that he might not pass the exam?

My heart started pounding harder as I struggled to understand what he was saying and why he was saying it. "Well, I am not going to fail," I said. I put my head down and ignored him for the rest of the evening. But my anger smoldered.

Only after we had both passed the bar exam did Peter and I discuss more rationally our different approaches to the possibility of failing. Peter explained that he preferred to brace himself for the worst and to be pleasantly surprised when things worked out well. I preferred the optimistic approach, assuming we would both pass the exam and dealing with failure if—and only if—the worst happened. This difference in perspective was a common thread through most of our arguments: both viewpoints were legitimate, but we nearly drove each other crazy trying to find commonality on many issues.

We differed in other fundamental ways: for example, we wanted to do different things with our time off. Peter wanted to read the *New York Times* and the *Wall Street Journal*. I wanted to ride my Arabian horse in the Oakland hills. He wanted to go to jazz clubs and listen to music. I wanted intimate restaurant dinners and conversation. I wanted to decorate our beautiful apartment with furnishings that, admittedly, we would have had to put on credit cards. Peter did not see the need for any furnishings and dug in his heels over spending money we had not yet earned. We quarreled in a department store over whether we should get an area rug. Our arguing continued unabated, and our intimate life deteriorated even further.

Of course, we had good times, too. We made some wonderful friends and enjoyed socializing with them. Especially after a few drinks, Peter and I found each other witty and amusing.

We could also see the humor in our missteps. Once, not long after we joined our firms, I had a minor surgical procedure and, in a rare break from work, was resting after returning home. I'd had a large intravenous sedative and was still woozy when the phone rang. A man with a heavy Swedish accent said, "Hello, this is Bjorn. Is Peter there?" I seemed to recall Peter saying something about someone visiting from Sweden, and I wanted to honor his wish to be welcoming. I invited Bjorn to stay in our small second bedroom, believing Peter would be happy that I got everything arranged.

Only after Peter had returned from work, the three of us had finished dinner, and I offered to get Bjorn some fresh towels did Peter look at me sideways and say, "Gail, may I talk with you for a moment?" We pushed back our chairs and had a little huddle in the hallway. "Who *is* this guy?" Peter asked.

"I thought *you* knew him," I said.

"No, I don't know him," Peter said, even more puzzled. "Is he staying here?"

"Yes," I shrugged, feeling helpless to do anything more.

Bjorn ended up staying for five days, and we all had a great time. But that's how Peter and I were. We tried to march to the same drummer, but we always seemed to miss a beat or two.

☙❧

One of the things I struggled with on a fundamental level was a tendency to be fearful in all sorts of situations. During my first marriage, a nurse was abducted at a nearby hospital and murdered. Her body was found in a field near our home. I was devastated for her and deeply frightened for my own safety.

Around the same time, I read *Helter Skelter*, and it upset me so much that I couldn't sleep well for a year. My first husband had been protective of me, but Peter did not have a protective bone in his body. He considered me an equal and a peer in all ways.

When Peter and I lived in San Francisco, I had a toy poodle named Thor. Thor needed to be walked several times a day; at night this involved walking through the dark basement of our building to the back yard before bed. Peter liked Thor (his mother once told me she knew Peter was in love when he walked a toy poodle in Texas). He even made up a silly song that he liked to sing to Thor. I no longer recall the tune or the lyrics, but the gist of the song was that Thor was a good dog, a sweet dog, a very good dog. Thor loved that song. He knew it was about him. Peter cheerfully walked Thor half of the days, and I did the other half. But at night I was afraid to go downstairs into the basement or to the park by myself. I had never conquered my childhood fear of the dark. Even if I had been more courageous, I didn't think it was safe for me to go out alone at night with only a toy poodle for protection. Peter thought it was fine for me to do so, and that our neighborhood was safe. But I had a deep desire to be protected and already suffered from feelings of abandonment. Peter loved me, but he seemed put off by my fears. I stuffed them down as best I could. When it was my turn to take Thor outside at night, I rode the elevator down to the lobby and unlocked the door into the pitch-dark basement. I shifted from foot to foot at the back door and tried to rush Thor, who, of course, wanted to linger. Yes, I walked my dog at night. But I was frightened and resentful.

My fears had possibly been blown out of proportion for reasons dating back to my childhood, and it was unlikely that a monster would attack me in the basement of our apartment building. But I knew that I faced *real* dangers that I wanted Peter to appreciate. One evening when I was returning to our apartment, a young man surprised me by pushing close behind me and entering our apartment building after I unlocked the door to the lobby. His manner unnerved me, and I quickly got into the elevator. The man squeezed in with me. Before he could close the door, I stepped out, bolted up four flights of stairs, and slipped, breathless, into our apartment, locking the door just as the elevator groaned to a stop at our floor. I heard the man get off the elevator and walk down the stairs outside our door, and I felt frightened and vulnerable. Even though I did not expect Peter to be with me every minute or to escort me about town, I tried to get him to understand that I was more vulnerable than he was—but I just couldn't break through to him.

Years later, Peter apologized to me and told our sons he had made a mistake to leave me unprotected. I deeply appreciated the apology. I had apologized to him for my many failings, too. Why do we resist admitting fault when, in the end, it feels great to let anger go? It's cathartic to clean the slate with a sincere apology.

৭7

Despite our different natures and frustrating lack of sync, Peter and I had some deeply bonding experiences, as well. Three years into our marriage, I was involved in a serious car accident. An associate from my law firm was driving my new car after a firm function, and I was his passenger. The associate lost control and hit a pedestrian on the steps of San Francisco's ACT Theater. The pedestrian was seriously injured: he lost his leg below the knee. The accident forever altered the injured man's life and threw my life into a tailspin of guilt and sorrow. Peter rose to the occasion to support me in that sorrow. I called him at midnight from a phone booth after the accident, waking him from a deep sleep. "Peter, I've been involved in a terrible accident," I sobbed. "A pedestrian was badly injured."

"Where are you?" he asked. "I'm coming to get you. I'll be right there." Peter must have sped over the Golden Gate Bridge. He drove up, jumped out of the car, and wrapped me in his arms. I have learned over the years that Peter is an amazing friend when the chips are down. The bigger the crisis, the steadier he becomes. I felt very close to him in the days after that terrible accident as we dealt with its human and legal ramifications.

$$\approx\!\!\Omega\!\!\Omega\!\!\approx$$

The car accident taught me some valuable lessons. First, of course, was the sickening wake-up call of being involved in a disaster that leaves another person—an innocent bystander—permanently maimed. Although I had not been driving, I'd exercised poor judgment by giving the keys to my car to an associate who had hosted a client dinner at a fancy restaurant in San Francisco. He lost control of the car on a street corner on Union Square, and catastrophe followed. The morning after the crash, a new wave of problems rained down on me. Days earlier, I had received a glowing annual review of my work for the third year in a row. My law firm told me I was doing everything right—and to just keep doing it. Now politics took over as the firm anticipated a huge lawsuit. Fears of a potential punitive damage award ran rampant amongst the firm partners. I wanted assurances of indemnification, but none were forthcoming. Everyone was too paranoid to admit the dinner had been a firm function. In our law firm, where the smallest tidbit of gossip ricocheted through the corridors at mach speed, the enormity of the car accident brought a pregnant silence to the hallways. No one dared speak of it as the partners convened behind closed doors with each other and wrangled with various insurance carriers. It was a long and stressful two years until the case finally settled.

My attorney—a senior litigator at Peter's firm—took us under his wing, and I experienced firsthand how critical it is to have an honest, capable attorney on your side in a high-stakes legal battle. (Nothing gives me more satisfaction as a lawyer than to give my clients confidence in the midst of a legal morass.) Days after the accident, with my attorney's blessing (and after his review), I sent a letter to the injured pedestrian at San Francisco General Hospital, where he was still recovering. I knew he had lost his leg, and I couldn't stand to let him wonder who had been in the car that had hit him. I met him in person many months later—after he had gotten his prosthesis. He was kind and forgiving and had appreciated my early letter. He could not possibly have been more gracious in receiving my heartfelt apologies, teaching me firsthand the true value of forgiveness.

My father was also deeply supportive after the accident. Although I hadn't been physically injured by the accident, I was emotionally devastated and could not eat or sleep for days. Dad and my sister Alice drove down to San Francisco from Seattle. They offered moral support and the love I dearly needed. Alice stayed on for awhile after my dad left. She fixed me soft-boiled eggs and toast—comfort food our mom used to make when we were sick. My mind was racing, and I asked her to read me Voltaire plays out loud. We were able to laugh a bit, but I was very low.

In the weeks following the car accident, my eating disorder reemerged. I was thirty years old and had been bulimic off and on for many years. Now I was experiencing the flip side of the disorder: anorexia. In anguish, I thought, "I have no control over what is happening. I don't know what to do. I can't eat.

Maybe I should get professional counseling and address this miserable eating disorder once and for all."

I made an appointment with a psychologist who specialized in eating disorders. I'd decided it was time to stop punishing myself. Through therapy I discovered many things, including that I had a naturally small appetite. My fears that I would balloon into obesity proved false; instead of gaining weight, I actually dropped a few pounds. I could hardly believe I was eating normally and was at last free of a disorder that had dogged me ever since I was a teenager. Ever since the car accident, whenever I've experienced a crisis in my life, I have tried to find a silver lining, and use crisis as an opportunity for growth. As my sister Linde says, "A kick in the pants is a kick in the right direction."

❧8

If there was one thing Peter and I were in perfect accord on, it was our desire to have children someday. After five years of marriage we decided "someday" had come, and we gave up our San Francisco apartment and bought a condo in Mill Valley to get ready for a life with children. When I became pregnant, we were thrilled. We happened to be taking ballroom dancing lessons at the time. We were enjoying them, so we kept up the lessons throughout my pregnancy. It got harder and harder for me to do the spins, and we laughed as Peter practically had to push me up the long staircase to the ballroom.

"I'm due next week," I told our group class, as we completed our lesson package. "My dancing days are over for awhile. But it's been fun."

"Well, *you* can still come, can't you?" a disappointed woman asked Peter. "Maybe not," she quickly said, hearing me gasp and catching her own faux pas. I forgave her indiscretion, knowing how hard men are to come by at dance studios.

❧❧❧

My pregnancy was a breeze, but I was nervous about child-birth and had no qualms about wanting an epidural. I knew that my mom and most women in her generation had used anesthesia for childbirth, and I didn't want that—but I also didn't buy into the heroic notion of natural childbirth. So Peter and I took Lamaze classes and got ready for the blessed event. My sister Linde came down from Seattle and helped me assemble and decorate a nursery. I sat there in the rocking chair after she left, marveling that a tiny human being would soon arrive and I would have a baby of my own.

The Friday night I went into labor, Peter and I dutifully counted time between the contractions before calling the doctor. Things were clipping right along, but when I called my doctor, neither he nor any of his partners was available. Peter and I needed to drive from Mill Valley across the Golden Gate Bridge to San Francisco to get to the hospital. My labor was intense, so we started off while the doctor's office tried to track someone down.

By the time we got to the hospital, I was in transition labor and the nurse said I was ready to deliver. It was too late for an epidural or any other pain medication. Peter stood by me, holding my hand and counting slowly as I panted and tried to take long, slow breaths. I held onto his hand for dear life. By the time the doctor rushed in, there was nothing to do but catch the baby and pose for a picture. Peter was on cloud nine as he counted toes and fingers and told me our baby boy was perfect, and was already looking around the room with curiosity. I was ecstatic as Peter spoke on the phone with relatives, reporting our news with joy. I told Peter I wanted to name the baby after him because he'd been so wonderful helping me through my natural delivery. He was touched because we'd never talked about naming the baby Peter Jr. But he was thrilled and, after asking me to sleep on it to be sure, we named Peter Jr. the next morning. To avoid confusion, we nicknamed him PJ, which we still call him even though he has been Peter to his friends since kindergarten.

Motherhood has been my greatest joy in life. And Peter and I were both deliriously happy having this adorable baby boy. But Peter's parents, who themselves had lost three babies to miscarriage after having Peter, were out-of-body excited. Never, ever on this planet have there been better grandparents. Peter's father passed away a few years ago and took a big chunk of my heart with him.

Peter's dad was calm and loving and always had a kind word for me. Sometimes he would call me on the telephone just to say, "You've been on my mind. How are you doing?" He spent hours holding our children on his lap, patiently following them on neighborhood excursions, and teaching them that their ideas mattered. Peter's mom also devoted herself to loving her grandchildren, knitting blankets, hand-stitching baby clothes and sewing hundreds of costumes. They showed up from Texas the day we brought PJ home from the hospital. It was Christmas Eve. Peter had picked his parents up at the airport, eager to show off our baby. I greeted them at the front door with a huge smile, holding their newborn grandson. They stood for a moment, awestruck.

Soon we were all huddled on the living room sofa. "Look at all that hair!" Peter's father exclaimed.

PJ examined everyone with large brown eyes as we passed him around to one another saying, "Objectively speaking, do you not believe this is the most beautiful baby in the world?"

ᘒ9

PJ quickly became addicted to the twenty-four-hour rocking chair treatment. I had taken a six-month maternity leave, but Peter had to go back to work. I would sit in the chair, rocking PJ, and think maybe I could put him in his cradle for a little while and take a shower or do the dishes. His little angelic face was peaceful as we rocked and he slept. I stood up, slowly tiptoed to the cradle, having already learned he could sense things when he was asleep, and ever so gently eased him onto the comfy mattress.

"WHAAAAAA!!!!!!!!" He turned purple and flailed. I snatched him back up, rushed to the rocking chair, plopped down, and he instantly stopped crying, happy again. Everything's fine. Just don't leave. Rock. This was fun, but I was also getting pretty exhausted from his nighttime sleeping pattern, which was to wake every hour on the hour and request room service. We soon got a live-in nanny. Over time, this raised difficult issues—partly because I didn't want to share my children's affections with another woman and partly because the nanny seemed to want to sabotage my confidence as a mother. But Peter and I both wanted dependable and consistent childcare while we worked, and we needed extra help.

Despite the challenges of combining our professions with parenthood, Peter and I were both head-over-heels in love with our little boy. We'd bundle him into his stroller on days off and take long walks in the parks or the San Francisco Arboretum. One day when PJ was about ten months old, Peter and I looked at each other as PJ did some adorable thing. "You know," I said, "If we're going to have another one, we should do it soon so they'll be close together in age. That would be fun for PJ."

"Okay," Peter said. "That would be cool." He loved being a dad.

It took a little while to get pregnant again, but we did. Then we decided we needed more room for our growing family. Peter's parents generously helped us with a down payment, and we bought a house in Mill Valley. It was a cozy, turn-of-the-century Victorian and was large enough to accommodate us and our live-in nanny, who had a school-age daughter of her own. We had been settled into the house a few months when Amy and Roy moved in across the street with their little boy, Travis, who would become PJ's closest friend. Amy, a beautiful former actress with keen intelligence and the soul of an angel, would become my closest friend and confidante.

PJ was a bundle of energy from the day he was born. He walked by the age of nine months and was able to run across a room by eleven months. He made Curious George seem like a couch potato. PJ wanted to see, explore and understand *everything*. Like all tots, this included touching everything within reach and cramming loose items into his mouth. Peter and I and the nanny took turns following him like a twenty-four-hour tag team. But PJ was constantly on the move. We hired a carpenter to install slide bolts high on the outside of the bathroom door so that PJ could not even get into the room, let alone the medicine cabinet, when one of us was not with him. We had an iron gate installed at the top of the stairway so PJ wouldn't fall down the stairs. We kept a chain on the inside of the front door so he wouldn't escape.

Despite our best efforts to protect him from all danger, we could not do so. One morning, PJ located a Tylenol bottle that Peter had accidentally left on the kitchen counter. When I discovered PJ on top of the counter with the open bottle, I couldn't tell if he had taken any pills. I first called Peter at work and then dialed the emergency room. The nurse had us count the pills and, because there was no way to tell whether PJ had taken any, she told us to bring him to the hospital for treatment—just in case. Peter raced from San Francisco and met me and PJ at the emergency room. When we arrived, PJ showed no sign of feeling unwell, but we couldn't take any chances. Peter was beside himself with anguish over leaving the Tylenol bottle on the counter—he'd been distracted by a bad headache. I was frustrated with Peter, but PJ had found the open bottle on my watch: he'd beaten me to the kitchen that morning. Besides, I saw no point in punishing Peter over a mistake—he was so upset already. In any event, we had more important things to do than point fingers.

The emergency room doctor first instructed us to get PJ to drink a foul-tasting charcoal medicine. PJ choked on the first sip and there was nothing to do but force him to drink the rest. The doctor then had us administer ipecac to induce vomiting. Poor PJ was utterly bewildered and violently ill, and Peter and I wanted to die. For years afterward, PJ struggled and resisted whenever we had to give him medicine. To make matters worse, he had to go to the hospital several times to have tubes placed in his ears, as well as to have his tonsils removed. Those experiences were wrenching for all of us, and they contribute to my feeling that parenting is, at times, the hardest job on earth.

Aside from those medical challenges, PJ enjoyed robust health and seemingly endless energy. Peter and I often took him for walks in Mill Valley, and he loved visits to the fire department. The firemen always gave him a little red fire helmet and let him climb up onto the engine and hold onto the steering wheel. Early one Sunday morning, when PJ was around two, we arrived at the firehouse, and PJ could barely contain his excitement. But the firehouse doors were locked. "Open the door!" PJ called out.

"I'm sorry," Peter explained, bending over our bewildered boy. "The firemen are sleeping. They aren't up yet."

"We can come back later," I said.

PJ's face crumpled with disappointment. He was not about to give up so easily. "OPEN THE DOOR!" he yelled.

Peter picked PJ up to soothe him, but PJ started flailing and kicking his legs. "OPEN THE DOOR! OPEN THE DOOR!" He screamed all the way home. I could not open the firehouse door, but I opened a book on discipline soon after that. I was far along in my pregnancy with our second child, Ben, and thought I needed to get my act together.

"When your child is disappointed," the author said, "gently but firmly explain to him that you understand how he feels but . . . blah, blah, blah."

"Yeah, right," I thought. "This guy has never dealt with a real kid." PJ had golden ringlets and huge brown eyes. He was the picture of innocence as he cavorted about. Once when he was three and we were at the airport, he started running out of the restaurant while we were waiting in line to pay for our food. I chased him and, after I caught him, said, "PJ, *why* do you run off like this? We get scared that we'll lose you."

"Don't worry, mama," he answered. "I was going to come back. I just wanted to meet some new people." PJ has always been like this: a curious, exploring adventurer.

Between commuting back and forth between Mill Valley and San Francisco and traveling further away for work, our lives were a whirlwind. Just after PJ turned two, Ben arrived on the scene. My labor went even faster this time. My doctor had told me to call his office when I had my first contraction and to then get in the car and head to the hospital. My mom was visiting; we had just finished dinner (and Peter had excused himself to go to bed and fight a migraine headache) when my labor started. I waited a little while to make sure it was the real deal, but it didn't take too many twinges to convince me. My labor consisted of one long, building labor pain with no breaks. At ten o'clock Peter and I flew across the Golden Gate Bridge. This time, my doctor was waiting for us.

"Quick," the doctor said to Peter, "Change into scrubs. We need to get her into the delivery room fast." Peter snatched the scrubs and stepped into the adjoining bathroom to change.

"I need to push!" I screamed.

"Come back out!" the doctor called to Peter. Peter lurched back through the door and within a minute the doctor held up the baby. Joy and relief washed over me. Once again, we were ecstatic with a beautiful baby boy.

Poor Peter was dogged by the migraine headache that had hit him earlier in the evening. My doctor prescribed a strong pain medication for him and sent him home. No sooner did he awaken the next morning than our nanny's mother had an immigration emergency and Peter had to rush to help her. For two days, Ben and I bonded in our hospital bed and entertained doting grandparents. Ben had lots of blond hair, and deep blue eyes. Peter and I both have brown eyes, but a recessive blue gene from our respective fathers had traveled through us to Ben. Our new baby was relaxed and contented. He loved to snuggle. I held and kissed Ben and softly sang Elton John's song, "Blue eyes, baby's got blue eyes." There is simply nothing like the bliss of holding a new human being in your arms and thinking, "I did this. This unique and perfectly formed person came from me. No one on earth can take this baby from me."

❧❧

PJ was not thrilled with the hubbub that surrounded Ben's arrival at our Mill Valley house a couple of days later. He'd been missing his mom and wondered who in the heck she was bringing into the fold. I placed Ben's baby seat on the table where we could all admire him. PJ walked slowly as he scanned the occupant of the baby seat. Peter and I and our mothers stood close by, ogling Ben with rapt smiles. Again we asked, "*Objectively speaking*, is this not the most beautiful baby in the world?"

PJ climbed up on a chair to get a closer look, and the others left us alone so the young brothers could become acquainted. PJ looked at the baby and then at me, back to the baby, and then back to me. I could see the wheels turning in his mind as he sized up this small intruder. It took awhile for PJ to appreciate the benefits of having a little brother, but soon enough he and Ben became fast friends. As soon as he could scoot on his stomach, Ben began following PJ everywhere. With his first steps, he made a beeline for PJ, who was asleep on the floor, and pounced on him. They laughed and wrestled and played. Ben became a fellow adventurer—and that has lasted to this day.

❧10

"I really want to write my dissertation and complete my doctoral degree," Peter would say from time to time.

"Why do you want to do that?" I'd ask. "You're a partner in a law firm. What good is a PhD to a lawyer?"

"But it's important to me. I went to so much work to get through all my coursework and oral exams. I will never feel good about myself if I don't finish what I started."

After much struggling and resistance to the idea, I realized that Peter needed to finish his degree and that I should not stand in the way of his doing so. Peter took a leave from his firm and, over the next year, wrote his dissertation. That was one of the happiest times in our marriage. Peter was pursuing a dream, and I was helping him do so. I edited the one thousand page finished product, and he dedicated it to me. PJ and Ben were five and three when we watched their dad, in cap and gown, receive his doctoral degree. But soon after graduation, Peter returned to work with a vengeance, and we reverted to our old patterns of juggling family responsibilities with the demanding practice of law.

❧❧❧

As the boys grew, Peter and I worked hard and spent as much time as possible with our sons—sometimes together, increasingly not. One or the other child would wake up in the middle of the night every night, and both were early risers. Peter and I were sleep-deprived and exhausted, so we often took turns spending time with the children. We had no time to spend alone with each other, and we both knew our marriage was slipping into a distant third place behind child-rearing and practicing law. For awhile, we tried to find time for each other by spending occasional weekends together at nice hotels. Those times were enjoyable, but we fell into a pattern of relying almost exclusively on such occasions to focus on our relationship. The rest of the time, we spent whatever energy we had after work caring for the children.

Increasingly, as the boys grew older, we spent weekend time with other couples with children so we and the kids could socialize with others. As a result, the occasional weekends Peter and I spent alone in the city grew fewer and farther between. Bit by bit, we began to lead separate lives. As Peter later described it, we had more of a child-rearing partnership than a true marriage. That didn't make us bad people or bad parents, but as a married couple, we were out of sync and losing ground.

❧11

Our first nanny, who I will call Sylvia, was not an American citizen. She was a quiet, middle-aged woman from Mexico. When we hired her, the laws had not yet changed to make it unlawful for employers to hire "illegal aliens." But Peter and I were concerned about and wanted to address the immigration issue, so we hired an immigration attorney. Sylvia spoke Spanish and was learning English. Peter and I hired a translator to discuss the logistics with her. We began the legal process of applying for residency for her and her small daughter. The attorney advised us that it was a long process that required a number of steps. The longest delay, he explained, was the wait to reach the top of the list once all other steps had been completed. We went through all of the legal steps, and Sylvia got on the list—a very long list at her level of priority—for a green card.

Sylvia worked hard and we clearly needed the help, but I struggled with sharing my children's affections. Sylvia was a highly organized person by nature, and she rearranged everything in the kitchen, which had become her domain. I cooked for the children on the weekends, but I had difficulty even finding the utensils I needed. Peter's parents visited us often and loved to cook, as well. They'd buy armloads of fresh fruits and vegetables at the farmer's market, and I was glad for the bounty. Peter's mom made jelly from the fruit growing on our plum trees, and his father baked delicious homemade breads that we all enjoyed. Given my crazy schedule, I acquiesced in the shopping, cooking and organization by others, and I became disconnected from my own kitchen.

Every weekday, and sometimes on weekends, I'd leave for work in the morning and return at night, freaked out over missing my boys. If PJ skinned his knee or bumped something, he often ran to Sylvia, and it upset me deeply because I was his one and only mommy. By this time, I felt terribly guilty for working outside the home and sorry for myself for missing special milestones. "Look," Sylvia might say when I got home from work, "PJ has a new tooth!" I would smile and clap, but on the inside I agonized. These should be *my* mommy moments. To make matters worse, I was bone-tired from work, traveling, and handling jury trials.

Like so many working moms juggling demanding jobs and small children, I knew I was not performing my best in either role. During the middle of one jury trial in Santa Cruz, a couple hours from home, I settled into my hotel room after driving through a hellish rainstorm. I unpacked my briefcases and began a frantic search for the trial exhibits I had assembled over the weekend. I needed them to cross-examine a witness first thing in the morning. Oops. I had left them on my desk at home. Fortunately, my paralegal's husband was willing to get up at four the next morning and drive the exhibits to Santa Cruz. That trial ended well, but I was coming undone. When I got home, exhausted and desperate to see the boys, they didn't squeal and jump for joy as I wanted them to do. They were used to my coming and going and preparing for trials. They were fine with it—but, increasingly, I was not.

From time to time, I told Peter that I wanted to come home and be with the children. He did not think that was fair. He said he had married me when I was a lawyer and that he would like to be home with the kids, too. After a couple of years, I said emphatically that I wanted to stay at home with the kids. I said they needed me. Peter said I could not provide anything to the kids that Sylvia was not providing. He meant child care, but I heard something else entirely. I was stunned and deeply hurt—then outraged. I lost my temper and, for the first time threw out the *D* word. "Well, then, I will *divorce you* and find a man who will let me stay home with my children," I screamed. Then I smashed my hairdryer down on the floor. Ben was sitting in an infant seat and the hairdryer ricocheted past his head. I went weak-kneed and scrambled to recover my temper. Sylvia was in the house and had overheard our argument. I had no privacy. She did our laundry, she prepared our food, she cared for my children. I loathed her presence in my home and my life. I felt true despair.

One evening soon after that argument, Peter came home from work and said he had received a call from the immigration lawyer and that Sylvia was approaching the top of the list. In order for her to get her green card, we had to sign an affidavit saying she would be employed by us when she was given her card. When Sylvia heard that she was nearing the top of the list and should hear good news within about a month, she was giddy with excitement. I was genuinely happy for her and her daughter. I was also ecstatic for myself because we needed to follow through with that damn green card before letting her go.

Unfortunately, Peter received a call several days later from the immigration attorney who said he had made a mistake. He apologized profusely, but said he had misread the paperwork and that Sylvia was still about a year from the top of the list. Peter and I were stricken, knowing how disappointed Sylvia would be. I was sorry we had ever started the green card process in the first place. But we called the translator to the house to explain what had happened, and we all sat down at the dining room table. As Peter spoke, Sylvia sat with a frozen, depressed face. Although she barely uttered a word, I sensed that she did not believe the explanation. The thought crept into my mind, "She thinks we did this to keep her working for us. She doesn't believe the explanation." What I did not know until later was that Sylvia blamed *me* for this turn of events and, from that moment on, I had a passive-aggressive enemy in my own home.

The next morning when I walked into the kitchen, I greeted Sylvia's back at the kitchen sink—and thus began her silent treatment of me. She stood sullenly. I greeted her pleasantly, and she muttered a monosyllable in return. At the same time, knowing it made me uncomfortable, she increased her attention to PJ and Ben, who already adored her. She was determined to punish me—in my own home and through my own children—for what she thought I'd done to her. I felt the rug going out from under my feet. I told Peter that Sylvia was mad at me and thought I was responsible for screwing up her green card. He was busy and preoccupied with other things and thought I was overreacting. He thought Sylvia was understandably disappointed, but I felt this woman's growing hatred for me.

One afternoon a few weeks later, I slipped away from work, desperate to see my children. When I came through the door, PJ did not run into my arms as I hoped he would. Instead, he lingered near Sylvia, saying they had a secret. My heart lurched. Sylvia was sweeping the floor and smirking. She said, "Yes, PJ and I have a secret."

I went into a panic. To my horror, PJ said he did not want to go on a walk with me because he wanted to stay with Sylvia. I was reduced to bribery: I asked PJ with forced enthusiasm if he wanted to go out for ice cream. His face lit up and I scooped both boys into the car. After stopping by the ice cream store, I began driving randomly, my heart pounding. I was forcing back tears and trying to conceal my fear from my little boys. I was afraid to leave them alone with Sylvia; I thought she might kidnap my sons and take them to Mexico where I could not find them. I was outraged that she was keeping a secret with my child. I begged PJ to tell me the secret and said he could not have a secret from me. But I couldn't elicit a satisfactory answer.

I called Peter and told him I was quitting my job. I didn't give a tinker's damn about Sylvia's green card. I called Peter's father and asked him to fly to San Francisco the next day. He did. God bless him. He looked after the boys, bringing peace and calm to our house while I exercised my long-held advance permission to quit my job if someone abused me. I never dreamed it would be our nanny. Nevertheless, I gave my law firm notice, and told Sylvia that I was coming home to take care of my children. We would no longer need her services.

❧12

When I came home from work to care for the boys, I thought life would be a bowl of cherries. How hard can it be to take care of a couple of kids? Within days, our laundry pile dwarfed Mount Everest. The dishes were pushing a close second. Plus, my law firm had rejected my resignation of partnership and given me a leave of absence. I continued to work for one Fortune 500 client from home. I hired help with running the house, figuring that would fix things. The boys were whirlwinds of activity—in and out of costumes all day long and back and forth to my neighbor Amy's. The playroom was well beyond my ability to keep organized, and the children tore it apart again every time I tried. I had new respect for women who "did not work" and merely ran households. I began spending lots more time with Amy. Let the laundry wait. Peter increased his already crazy work schedule. He may have been angry with me for abandoning him to the role of sole provider while I got to stay home with the kids, but I felt I had earned the right to be there. I had carried these little boys and given birth to them—and I didn't care who was mad at me for staying home.

ॐ२ॐ

Despite my determination to morph into a domestic goddess, after practicing law for so many years, I struggled to gain proficiency in the role of stay-at-home mom. So I resorted to certain efficiencies to save time. One of them was bathing the boys together. One Sunday morning when PJ and Ben were five and three years old, I ran a bathtub full of water for the boys while I blow-dried my hair. Peter had just left to go to the gym and wouldn't be home for a couple of hours. PJ was sitting in the tub with a flotilla of plastic boats when Ben strode into the room, shedding his clothes and preparing to sling a leg over the side of the tub.

"I want to have my own bath," PJ said. Ben froze. But I thought PJ's request sounded reasonable enough. We had no plans that morning. I could easily run Ben his own bath when PJ was finished.

"Okay, PJ," I said. "You can have your bath next," I said to Ben.

Ben tried to hurtle over the side of the tub. "I don't want to wait!" he wailed. "I want my bath now!"

I put down the hair dyer and caught hold of Ben, pulling him back from the tub and setting him on the floor. "Ben, you can have your bath next. PJ wants to have his own bath this morning."

Again Ben tried to plunge into the tub where PJ's floating boats bobbed in the bubbles. I gently but firmly pulled him from the tub—just like the textbooks instruct you to do—and said, "If you can't be nice, Ben, you'll have to wait outside the bathroom for your turn." I eased him outside the bathroom door, taking care to see that his flailing arms and grasping fingers were not pinched in the door as I calmly pushed it shut.

There was a dead silence on the other side of the door. PJ and I looked at each other. We then heard the sound of Ben's little bare feet running away. He'll go console himself somewhere and think about his lesson in being patient, I thought. Just like those parenting books say children do. But soon we heard the little running feet coming back our direction. There was a scritch-scratching sound on the other side of the door followed by the thud of a sliding bolt. *Uh oh.* I turned off my hairdryer and set it down on the counter. That sounded like the old deadbolt we put on the outside of the bathroom door to keep the kids out of the medicine cabinet. We hadn't used it in a long time. I put my hand on the doorknob and tried to open the door, but it wouldn't budge. I chuckled in disbelief. Surely Ben wouldn't lock us in the bathroom, would he?

"You don't have any friends and I'm never letting you out!" Ben yelled as if reading my mind. PJ and I locked eyes as we heard Ben's little feet running away again. I rattled and pulled on the bathroom door.

"Ben!" I called out. No answer. I pressed my ear to the door and heard muffled noises in the kitchen that sounded like a chair scraping along the floor. Has he climbed up on the counter out there? Is that the sound of the candy jar opening? "Ben! Come here!" I called. Slowly, I heard little feet wandering my direction. "Ben," I said. "What are you doing out there?"

"Nuffing," he answered. He could barely speak through his mouthful of candy.

"Unlock the door, Ben." I kept my voice even. "Please unlock the door."

I heard some half-hearted scritch-scratches on the other side of the door. "I can't reach it," Ben said. True enough. The deadbolt was high up on the door, and I didn't know how he'd managed to reach it in the first place. But locking it was clearly easier than unlocking it would be.

"Do you think we'll ever get out of here?" PJ asked. His water was cooling, and the bubbles were stretching out and flattening. His plastic boat flotilla bobbed listlessly.

"Sure," I said. "I just don't know when." I opened the bathroom window and leaned out. It was a two-story drop to a concrete walk below. The neighbor's orchard beyond the fence was empty and quiet.

"Ben? Where are you?" I thought I heard the front door slam. Then silence.

PJ climbed out of the tub and wrapped himself in a towel. As I paced the bathroom and worried about what to do, the phone started ringing in my study. I could hear my voice on the recorded message before Amy's voice came onto the message machine. I pressed my ear against the door, straining to hear.

"Hi, Gail. It's Amy. Ben just arrived naked with the puppies (our two cocker spaniels), and I thought I'd check in and see what you're up to. Give me a call." Beep.

Ben had crossed the street alone with our two puppies! "Okay, Amy. Figure it out," I said. PJ and I waited longer. After awhile, the telephone rang again. I knew it would be Amy.

"Hi Gail. It's Amy again." She sounded relaxed but curious. "Ben and the puppies are still here and we're happy to have them, but I thought we should touch bases."

"Come on, Amy!" I called through the bathroom door toward the answering machine.

"I think I'll send Roy over to see what's up." Yes!

"Yay!" PJ jumped up and down.

I raced to the window, and in a couple of minutes I could hear Roy's voice in the distance. "Roy!" I screamed.

"What? What? Where are you?"

"We're locked in the bathroom!" Within moments, Roy was on the other side of the bathroom door.

"I don't understand how you managed to do this," he said as he unlocked the bolt. He opened the door to find me standing in my bathrobe with my hands on my hips and PJ shivering in a towel. He shook his head. I looked down at Ben, who was standing next to Roy, naked—with remnants of candy smeared all over his face.

"I cricked you," Ben said. Then he smiled.

I smiled back. I couldn't help it. He *had* cricked me. (On Halloween Ben said, "Crick or Creat.") He also spelled his name N-E-B.

I remembered that my dad used to call me "Bag of Tricks" or "BT" when I was small. He would say, "You are always up to a trick!" because I loved to play little pranks on my family members—and so did Ben. I don't easily get angry with any of my kids but, of all of them, when Ben looks at me with those twinkling eyes, he just slays me; he can get away with anything. So, even after locking me and PJ in the bathroom for an hour, raiding the candy jar, and visiting the neighbors au naturel, he was able to disarm me with a single smile.

❡13

Peter and I wanted to raise the kids to have good morals, and we taught them the usual social conventions and rules. I found these took at least one thousand repetitions per kid. But neither Peter nor I were church-goers, and we shared a laissez faire attitude toward religion. We had both been raised as Episcopalians, but under different circumstances. Peter's parents had attended services regularly when Peter was young, and his mother still thought going to church was important. But his father had long since stopped going. In a relaxed manner, he said he simply didn't believe. He had a beautiful tenor voice and still enjoyed singing hymns, however.

My father left the Catholic Church at the age of twelve and refused to return; his dad never forgave him for doing so. My parents had to elope because my mom was a Protestant. Throughout our youth and adulthood, Dad ranted about the Church, calling it "that Black Roman outfit." I can only speculate as to what precipitated my father's break with the Catholic Church, but I often wonder if he was one of the young boys who fell victim to sexual abuse. Even if true, that would not excuse his berating everyone who attended church or had any spiritual beliefs at all. I found it all bewildering. I was baptized as a baby, and my mother took me to the Episcopal Church to become confirmed when I was twelve, but we only loosely attended services. I wanted a spiritual connection, but couldn't force myself to believe much of the creed.

Nonetheless, I still longed for a connection with my creator, and thought I would learn something through going to church. I was reading spiritual literature on my own and was open to growth. In particular, I loved *The Gospel According to Jesus*, by Stephen Mitchell, a Jewish scholar who brought Jesus to life for me more vividly than ever before. I also loved *Sermon on the Mount*, by Emmett Fox, who also captured the spirit of love I sensed in Jesus. How I longed to have sat on the edge of the mountain and to have heard Jesus speak. I befriended a wonderful woman who was an Episcopalian minister.

"I need to find God," I explained.

"Don't worry," she answered. "God will find you." I took great comfort in her words. But I felt ill-equipped to ground my children in worship. Frankly, I had no clue how to go about it. But Peter and I decided to make an effort to expose them to Christianity, and we identified Grace Cathedral in San Francisco as a place to start.

One Sunday morning when the boys were about six and four, Peter woke up at six o'clock and hopped out of bed to head to work, as usual. I rose on one elbow to say goodbye, and Peter asked me if I wanted to bring the boys into San Francisco to go to Grace Cathedral for the eleven o'clock service. I yawned and said that sounded fine. Peter then dressed in a suit and headed for the office.

I got up around seven thirty with PJ and Ben and let them watch cartoons after breakfast. They happily lay on their stomachs in the living room as I made some coffee and wandered into my study, where I had a new computer. I started fooling around writing a story and soon disappeared into a fictional world, loosely based on my own childhood. I thundered away on the keys. I fixed a couple more cups of coffee and sat thinking about my story while the boys concentrated on their cartoons. Suddenly, as I sipped my coffee, my eyes fell on the clock— it was ten thirty. I panicked and bolted out of the chair, catching sight of myself in the mirror. I looked like a deer in the headlights with my hair standing straight up. Peter would be standing on the steps of Grace Cathedral, waiting for us, in thirty minutes. The drive into the city would take that long. I ran from the study into the living room, startling the boys, who rolled over onto their sides with wide eyes.

"We have to go to church!" I screamed. Having never been to church, this was a bit of a surprise to them. "Hurry up and get dressed! You have to put on suits!"

I shooed them toward their rooms, ordering them to show up in the living room—on the double—fully dressed. Then I turned and ran to my room. I leaped into a dress and full-length coat and, looking in the mirror at my hopeless hair, pulled on a hat. Then I ran back out to the living room where the bewildered boys—amazingly—showed up in their suits (or something resembling them).

I ushered them out to the car and we peeled out of the driveway, headed for San Francisco. I sped across the Golden Gate Bridge, telling the boys I was sorry to have lost track of time, but we were meeting Dad at church and it would be really fun. Sorry for the hurry. I zoomed up Lombard to Van Ness, tore up Nob Hill and made the turn in front of Grace Cathedral on two wheels. There I saw Peter pacing at the top of the steps and looking at his watch. I opened the door, sent the boys running to Peter, and jumped back in the car to park. I don't know what sense of urgency possessed me, but I couldn't control myself. I crammed the car into drive and tore around the corner into a parking garage across from the cathedral. The garage attendant looked at me through sleepy eyelids. "That will be five dollars," he said. When I handed him my credit card, he said, "We only accept cash."

"I don't have cash and I am trying to go to church!" I yelled.

"Well, we don't take credit cards."

I crammed the car into reverse and smashed my foot on the pedal, roaring backwards up the long ramp to the street. When I finally found a parking spot some blocks away, I held onto my hat and ran to the church. Peter and the boys were kneeling together at the communion bench while all of the other children were in Sunday School. When I finally arrived and squished myself into line to have a gulp of wine, PJ, on his knees, slid his eyes sideways at me with a look that asked, "What exactly are we doing here?"

My sister, Alice, had also been taking her children to church, and she had better success, although her children had questions, too. One Memorial Day Sunday, she took her little daughter to the Episcopal Church, and as they entered the sanctuary, my niece pointed to a list of names displayed on a board. "What's that?"

"That's a list of men from this parish who've died in the service," Alice whispered.

There was a long pause before my wide-eyed niece asked, "The nine o'clock or the eleven o'clock?"

⚬⚬⚬

I am afraid our early ventures to church added more confusion than comfort to our son's lives. At our house, as in so many others, Christmas was all about Santa Claus. When PJ was six, we were riding in the car one day, and he began assaulting me with questions.

"Is Santa Claus real?" he asked.

Uh oh, I thought. He's too young to know the truth. I'll brush this off for now. "*I* believe he's real," I said, crossing my fingers and remembering my mother's instructions about certain harmless lies being okay.

"But how can *one man* take toys to every kid in the whole world?" PJ pressed.

"Well, he does it in his sleigh with all the reindeer. It's magic," I answered.

"Reindeer can't fly. And how could Santa Claus get down the chimney with all those presents?"

I felt my confidence in white lies slipping, but I dodged and parried his questions until finally we drove up in front of our house.

"*You* are Santa Claus, aren't you?" he asked with all the vigor of Clarence Darrow. I crumbled under the pressure, my head falling onto my hands on the steering wheel.

"Yes," I said in a tiny voice. The silence that filled the family van was deafening. I lifted my head and turned to look at PJ. The shock registering on his face instantly told me I had made a terrible mistake. I wanted to take back my words but, as I searched vainly for some explanation, PJ broke the silence.

"I'm going to tell Ben," he said.

"Oh, no you're not," I said.

"Yes, I am."

"No, you're not." This was going nowhere, but we carried the discussion into the house. I couldn't get the upper hand. Mercifully, Ben was napping, and PJ and I sat down in the living room.

"I'm going to tell Ben when he wakes up," PJ said. "I have to tell him."

In one of my lowest moments as a mother, I said, "If you tell Ben, then Santa Claus won't bring you any presents."

PJ looked crushed for a moment, but then a light gleamed in his six-year-old eyes. "I don't care," he said. "Because I'm Jewish. And I'll just celebrate Hanukkah. They get presents every day for a whole week."

"You are not Jewish," I said. "Because I am not Jewish."

"I don't care if you're Jewish," he said. "I'm Jewish."

"You can't be Jewish," I said. "You have to be *chosen* to be Jewish."

Finally, the air sagged out of him and a defeated PJ said, "I guess I wasn't choosed." We sat in a silent stand-off.

"Well," I finally said, "I believe that Santa Claus is real. And I think you and Ben should believe he is real, too." PJ nodded and that was the end of that.

Several days later, we flew to Peter's parents' home in Texas for Christmas. On Christmas day, Peter's mother asked PJ to go to church with her and help serve Christmas dinner to the homeless.

"I don't want to!" he wailed.

"Why, PJ?" Peter and I asked. "You will be helping less fortunate people."

"Because everyone there knows what they believe, and I don't know what I believe!"

He was finally persuaded to go and, even if he did not settle on his spiritual beliefs that evening, he was glad he helped serve the meals.

PJ, now an agnostic, has always cared deeply for the suffering masses. He astounded me once when I was reading him *The Black Stallion*. "Let's look at the atlas," I said, "to see where Alex and his dad were sailing off the African coast."

As I searched for the route the fictional characters were taking, PJ ran his finger over Ethiopia on the map. "This is a zone of pain," he said.

Startled, I looked where he pointed and then asked him, "What do you mean? Why did you say that?"

"Because the people there are suffering so much," he answered. He was nine years old, and I had no idea where he had picked this up.

Not long ago, PJ (then twenty-five and living in California) told me he'd served Sunday breakfast at a downtown Los

Angeles homeless shelter. He'd cracked hundreds of eggs while elbow-to-elbow with other folks doing community service.

"What prompted you to do it?" I asked, pleased that he'd made the effort.

"My life in West Hollywood is fun, but it can be a bit shallow. Everyone is focusing on how they look when there is so much suffering nearby. I just wanted to help out."

❧14

Shortly after I left work to be with the kids, my father came to visit me and Peter and the kids. Dad's longtime companion, Anita, was with him. Anita, a woman younger than I am (nearly thirty years younger than my dad) is a lovely woman, whom my siblings and I consider an honorary sister. She once described my father as "exasperating," rolling her eyes and laughing when she said this. Even Dad thought that was a hilarious understatement. But there was nothing funny about this visit.

Mr. Hyde was in the driver's seat from the time my dad and Anita arrived. I was in the kitchen preparing a huge and festive meal while the boys bounded around the house, excited by all the activity. While I was trying to concentrate on the menu, my father started telling me a sexually explicit story—and I cut him off. If there was one thing my father hated his children to do, it was to cut him off in the middle of a story. He started up again and I turned my back on him and started talking to Anita about something else. The dinner went reasonably well until Peter and the kids finished and excused themselves, leaving me to visit with Dad and Anita. As we lingered over coffee, my father began criticizing my mother, as he often did, to my immense discomfort. After he droned a litany of accusations against my mother (going back to their dating years), I finally mustered up the guts to say, "You have to stop talking to me this way. It's making me ill."

This did not slow him down. Instead, he raised his voice and continued his criticisms of Mom, who had long since remarried and enjoyed a life of comfort my father probably envied. He made up ugly stories out of whole cloth. As his comments became increasingly fanciful and vicious, I felt even sicker, as though I were complicit in the lies my father was forcing down my throat.

I loved both my parents, and that night, as my father said vicious things about my mother, I felt I should be strong enough to defend her. After years of relief from bulimia, I felt as though I might vomit. But rather than rise bravely to my mother's defense, I slumped lower in my chair and said in a small, pleading voice, "Did you know I was bulimic for thirteen years? You must stop talking to me like this. It's making me ill."

My father actually did stop talking, and he stared at me. I had never told him about my eating disorder. I could see the wheels turning in his mind as his face settled into a defiant mask. "Your mother *never loved you*," he finally said with great deliberation. "That is your problem."

"You have to stop doing this to me," I said weakly. "It's killing me." I felt the life sagging out of me.

"Well, I don't know what to tell you," he said. "Because it's true."

My father may as well have plunged a butcher knife into my heart. Of course I knew—intellectually at least—the pure falsity of what he had said. My mother was not perfect, and she may not have loved him, but she had always loved me. I later thought I should have kicked him out of my house right then. I re-ran the incident in my mind and changed the ending. In my fantasized version, I marched down to the end of the table and grabbed all 200-plus pounds of him by the neck and kicked him out my front door. I pummeled him in the street. I screamed like a wild woman. But what really happened is that I slunk off to bed and curled into a shaking little ball. In the morning, I crept into my own kitchen like a trembling leaf while my father drank coffee and acted like nothing had happened. He'd slept like a baby and showed no glimmer of compunction over the destructive things he'd said to me. Poor Anita was devastated, and she simply hugged me tight with sympathy when they finally walked out my front door. Not long after, Anita left my Dad. They had been together for seventeen years.

This incident was the beginning of the end of my taking that kind of treatment. I was flooded with memories of things my father had said and done in the past, and felt caught in a powerful current of emotion that frightened me. I was no longer willing or able to pretend that everything was alright. I began working closely with a therapist and planning to confront my father. All of the molten lava that had been smoldering in me for decades began stirring and threatening to erupt. I was coming unglued emotionally and asked my therapist how long it would take me to resolve these issues, hoping to write down a date on my calendar when I would be whole and healed—preferably by the following week.

"It usually takes two years of therapy to deal with these kinds of issues," My therapist said.

"What?" I gasped. "Two years? I don't have two years!" I told my therapist I needed a faster plan. But she just gave me a sad, knowing smile, and I soon learned that progress came at a significantly slower and less predictable rate than I'd hoped. I could not advance as quickly as I wanted. I was a pretty good actor, though, after practicing repression for so many years. I got out of bed each morning and functioned well on the surface even though I was a mess inside. It still makes me sad to think of it, because I was so preoccupied and sick that often I couldn't be fully present for the boys. They would say, "Look, mommy!" as they cavorted about. I'd want to focus on them and really connect, but I was too ill to fully relax and enjoy these simple moments in life.

As I struggled to run the household, and grappled with these personal issues in therapy, my sister, Linde, gave me some helpful parenting advice. Years earlier, when her children were small, she'd found a wonderful pediatrician named Dr. Van Passion. (It was spelled differently, but this was the way I always imagined it.) Dr. Van Passion said that the one essential ingredient to raising healthy kids was to love them unconditionally and to let them know every day that, if you had to do it all over again, you would have them and love them with all your heart. Peter and I had that part nailed. But beyond that, there were some other guidelines that proved helpful. One was to pick your battles. Dr. Van Passion advised parents not to make a bunch of rules (eat your peas, make your bed, whatever), but to have just a few and to really enforce them. (Many years later, I came across an article about Dr. Van Passion's adult son, who had become a successful businessman and philanthropist, validating the success of his father's approach to child-rearing.) This approach worked for me by nature and also fit well into our lifestyle. I didn't want to be nagging my kids over minutia, but I wanted them to grow into responsible adults and good people. My growing boys gave me plenty of opportunities to test the doctor's advice.

Ben was easygoing and soft-spoken, but he also had a strong personality and was no pushover. He put me to the test on the topic of picking battles when he was in preschool. Ultimately, we both won, I think.

Ben liked the freedom of dressing light. For awhile, his preferred outfit was a pair of extremely short shorts and tennis shoes—with no socks. Before Ben started preschool, he had a large assortment of pants, shirts, coats, sweatshirts and socks. Mill Valley had a pretty balmy climate, but I balked when Ben insisted on wearing short shorts and tennis shoes with no socks the first day of preschool. Ben was determined to wear what he wanted to school. On the other hand, I was on the board of the preschool, and I had a reputation of sorts to protect. So I forced him to wear more normal clothes. For several days, each time I got Ben ready for school, we had a battle over his outfit, and we both had terrible, tumultuous starts to our day.

I started thinking about Dr. Van Passion's advice about picking your battles. On day four, I told Ben to go get dressed while I made his breakfast. Soon afterward, he walked into the kitchen in short red shorts and tennis shoes (no socks). I winced, but gave him his cereal and walked to his room while he ate. I got an armload of clothes out of his closet and put them in the car. At that time, we were giving one of Ben's schoolmates a ride to school with us. Casey showed up in a normal outfit, looking appropriate, and I felt a little weird when I buckled them into the car. Casey was dressed in jeans and a fall jacket. Ben looked like he was headed to the swimming pool.

When we arrived at school, I told the teacher and headmistress that Ben and I had been battling over his clothing and that it was wrecking both our days. I told them I was putting a bunch of clothes in his cubby (partly to prove he actually had appropriate clothing) and said I would be letting him dress himself from now on. If he decided he was cold or wanted to look normal, he could get some clothes out of his cubby.

Every day, Ben went off to school wearing variations on the same clothes. After a few months, the time came for parent-teacher conferences and I dreaded it, knowing the teachers must think I couldn't even dress my own kid. When the appointed time arrived, I went to the school and perched on a miniature chair at a table near the finger paints. The wait was a bit nerve-wracking, and I sat with my hands clutched in my lap. Finally the headmistress and Ben's teacher sat down in equally tiny chairs across from me. They were kind, loving women. One of them started speaking. "Do you know that Ben is very . . . " I hung on her words. " . . . popular?" she asked.

"Popular?" I blinked. Of course I thought my son was adorable, but I had never even considered the concept of popularity.

At home, he was just one of four boys running back and forth between our house and Amy's.

"Yes," Ben's teacher said. "Every day we have to reorganize the lunch table because everyone wants to sit next to Ben."

I stared at her, taking this in and thinking about Ben. Sweet Ben. Soft-spoken Ben who knew what he wanted to wear.

The headmistress smiled. "Everyone wants to wear shorts and no one wants to wear socks," she said. I bit my lip and held back a laugh. "But we found a way to get around the socks issue," she said. Ben's teacher, Margaret, was an ethereally pretty young woman, and Ben adored her. "Margaret told Ben the girls wouldn't like him if his feet were dirty," the headmistress explained, "and so he agreed to wear socks."

"I'm amazed," I said. "Do you know what he's doing to make everyone like him so much?"

"We don't, actually," the headmistress said. "We've talked about it amongst ourselves. He's imaginative and nice to the other children, but there is just something about him. The other kids want to be with him and to be like him."

This beautiful quality of Ben's has endured to this day. People have always liked and been drawn to him. He still has a distinctive idea of how he wants to dress (although his choices now please me). But the moral of the story for me was that Dr. Van Passion's advice was solid. Pick your battles. I didn't like sending Ben off to preschool in his wacky short shorts because I felt embarrassed. But Ben knew who he was, and he had a magic that could have been squashed if he'd been forced to wear clothes he hated.

❧15

After much planning and work with my therapist, I drove from Mill Valley to Seattle with my young sons. I'd called my dad and told him I wanted to meet with him privately. We sat down at his kitchen table and, for the first time in my life, I demanded that he observe boundaries with me and my family. I told him he could not talk to me about sex, religion or my mother—ever again. He sat silently, as I had requested, but I could tell he was not really listening. I may as well have been telling a tsunami to stay offshore. My father could not—or would not—observe boundaries. But I meant business. I wasn't going to take it anymore. Since he didn't clearly agree to my terms, I cut off contact with him. I headed back to California with my boys feeling terrified of how my father might react to my rejection. For months, I'd find myself speaking in a whisper whenever his name came up. He was eight hundred miles away, but always hovered in the shadows of my mind.

Peter was working almost all of the time, and I did not talk with him too much about my issues with my father. By the time PJ and Ben were six and four, I was lonely and struggling with unhappiness in my marriage and my life in general. I hadn't seen my father in several years. My mom and siblings were all supportive, but didn't have any fixes; it was a sad state of affairs. Peter tried to be supportive when he was home, but no one could fill the kind of void I felt. I began thinking that another baby would help. More accurately, I longed from the depths of my soul for a daughter.

PJ had recently been telling me that he and Ben wanted a baby sister. In fact, he had been telling me that for several years. I began imagining how wonderful it would be to have a little girl to go with our boys. I pictured a girl with oceans of curls and big brown eyes. Now, one may ask, "Why did you want another baby if you were struggling and unhappy in your marriage?" Okay, fair enough. I did get the beautiful daughter I wanted, with oceans of hair and big brown eyes. But no, she didn't fix things between me and Peter, and a baby cannot fill a big void in anyone's life. I would do it again without hesitation, but I join the long list of people who can attest that babies are not problem-fixers. That being said, our daughter, Leigh, is joy personified, and Peter and I and our sons cannot even imagine our lives without her.

Leigh was born six months before I turned forty. Peter and I pulled together again to share that ecstatic feeling accompanying the arrival of a new child. *Objectively speaking*, she was the most beautiful baby in the world! When Leigh was an infant, we hired Amy's niece, a cheerful and energetic college student, to help me with the children. I continued working part-time from home for my long-term corporate client; it was low-key, low-pressure work a few hours a week. I loved keeping that connection with the practice of law while raising my kids.

Not long after Leigh was born, that situation changed dramatically: my client suffered a devastating adverse judgment in a product liability case in San Francisco. An avalanche of lawsuits began against them, and it was "all hands on deck" for their lawyers. "We need your help," the general counsel said.

I reminded him that I was at home with my kids, and he said that was no problem as long as I continued working as much as I could. The client started sending boxes of documents from the company's headquarters in the Midwest to my house. As boxes piled up in the living room, I knew I needed to hire lawyers and paralegals to help me with the work. I leased a contemporary house just five minutes from my home and set up an unconventional law office. I hired several attorneys and paralegals and took the plunge back into full-tilt work, as thousands of lawsuits poured in from around the country. I worked closely with the general counsel, flying back and forth across the country every couple of weeks. Peter, meanwhile, opened the San Francisco office of a large Seattle firm and continued working at a breakneck pace.

Soon after I started my law firm, my sister, Linde, began working with me, commuting between Seattle and Mill Valley (her two kids were grown). She flew back and forth, ran the office and acted as my head paralegal and financial guru at the office, as well as my emotional supporter at home. Life in our household was pretty much a three-ring circus. My income and anxiety level shot up in unison.

Peter and I both wanted to be attentive parents, and we did a pretty good job, despite our crazy schedules. Linde lived with us part-time and helped us with the kids. Peter was working downtown full time, and I was traveling back and forth between my Mill Valley office, home, and Michigan. I ran through Chicago O'Hare like the White Rabbit on many occasions, looking at my watch, dragging my briefcase and frantically trying to catch my plane home. Even though I was my own boss, it was as hard as ever being both a mommy and a lawyer. Like working parents around the world, I didn't want to miss birthday parties, school plays, growth spurts, or hugs goodnight.

On one occasion, Peter and I were both traveling on business and needed to rendezvous in Seattle for some family occasion. Peter was flying from Boston, I was flying from Michigan, and Linde was coming from Mill Valley and bringing all three kids. The three planes were landing within a short time of each other. Linde was feverishly trying to finish some work at the office a few hours before her plane was scheduled to leave San Francisco. The babysitter called her nearly in tears.

"What's the matter?" Linde asked.

"Ben refuses to get dressed!" Ben was now five and still had strong ideas about his wardrobe, although he had branched out from short shorts.

"Put him on the phone," Linde said. "What is wrong?" Linde asked when Ben got on the line. "Why won't you get dressed?"

"Because PJ has new clothes and I look like a dick," Ben said.

"You look like what?"

"I look like a dick," Ben repeated. (Let me assure you that he did not learn this word at home. It must have been playground talk at the time.) In any event, Linde did not think Ben should have to feel that way about his clothing.

"Well, what do you want to wear?" she asked.

"I want the same clothes PJ is wearing."

Linde said she'd be there shortly to pick him up. She called me in Michigan to bring me up to speed and then dropped everything to take Ben shopping. Peter and I flew into Seattle and met Linde's plane. When PJ and Ben walked off the plane with matching outfits, Linde and I just looked at each other, shook our heads, and smiled.

"I wasn't going to make him wear clothes that made him feel like a dick," she later told me. "I just couldn't do it."

Ben and I didn't have any more fights over clothes. One day when I was very pregnant with our daughter, he came to me and asked if he could cut up a shirt so he could look like Michael Jackson. I had no idea what he was talking about, but I helped him select an old shirt and let him whack off a sleeve and cut a bunch of holes in it. He was satisfied and put it on just before I headed off with him to do some grocery shopping. As we turned the corner of a long aisle in Costco, I practically bumped into a CNN camera crew.

"Hi," said a heavily made-up guy standing in front of the camera.

"Hi," Ben and I answered.

"We're doing a show on warehouse club stores and wonder if we can follow you around and ask you some questions while you shop."

"Sure," I said. "No problem."

The CNN crew followed us all around Costco with cameras rolling as I loaded my cart and explained to them how I liked to cook lots of dinners and freeze them. I was the perfect housewife and mom. When we got into line, they turned off the camera and the news guy looked at my loaded cart and leaned close to me so no one else could hear. He cleared his throat and said, "Your son needs a new shirt."

I cracked up and told him that my son had designed that shirt and liked it just fine. Soon after I got home, while unloading the groceries, I called out to Amy in her front yard. "Hey, guess what? I was interviewed by CNN at Costco!"

"Ha ha, Miss Thang," Amy called back. "Did you tell them a nanny does all your cooking?"

I laughed and hauled all my stuff inside. Pretty soon the phone started ringing; I could hardly discern the screaming through the line. I finally recognized Amy's voice: "Turn on CNN! Turn on CNN!"

I grabbed my television control and flipped the channel to *CNN Headline News*. There I was, hugely pregnant with no makeup, alongside my little son who was wearing a mutilated shirt. Over and again, all day long, CNN played the clip about the mom shopping at Costco to save money and take care of her family. Well, I do like to cook yummy food and freeze it. But millions of people saw Ben in his cut-up shirt and probably thought I was a pretty neglectful mom. Oh well, Ben thought he looked good and, after all, that's what counts.

❧16

One day I got a call from Sylvia's employer saying that Sylvia had reached the top of the list for her green card. My stomach dropped. Why was she calling me? "There is one glitch," she said. "Sylvia can only get her green card if you and your husband sign an affidavit swearing that she is working for you, and that you intend to keep her in your employ."

No way, I thought. "I need to talk with my husband," I said before hanging up the telephone. The timing could not have been worse. I was under relentless pressure at work and juggling everything at home. I was in therapy and feeling insecure about everything. The last thing I wanted was to deal with Sylvia again. Despite her situation, I was determined to keep her out of our lives. I tried calling Peter at his office, but couldn't get through, so I leapt into my car and sped across the Golden Gate Bridge, headed for his office. My car phone wasn't working, and I careened into a couple of parking lots trying to call Peter from phone booths. I was frantic to tell him Sylvia *absolutely could not* care for our children again. When I couldn't get through on the phone, I kept on driving like Steve

McQueen up and down the hills of San Francisco until I parked underneath Peter's office building. I rode the elevator to the top and burst through the lobby of his firm and into his office. To say he was startled to see me barrel through the door is an understatement but, as I have said, crisis is his strong suit.

"Sylvia is at the top of the list, but she cannot come back into our house or take care of our children. There is no way. No way. Do you hear me?" I was breathless and panting.

Peter quickly sized up the situation and told his secretary, who was standing with a gaping jaw, that he and I were going to lunch. As we walked to the restaurant, I continued with a nonstop stream of words. Over lunch, Peter said, "I understand how you feel, but Sylvia did work hard for us and she and her daughter have a once-in-a-lifetime chance to get legal residency in the United States. The laws have changed and this is it. This is their one shot."

"I know that," I said. "But I am not going to have her in my house taking care of my children."

"It doesn't have to be for long," he said. "Just think how we'll feel if after all this time she loses her one chance. We can hire her in good faith and have my parents come out and stay with us so you feel okay."

Ultimately, Peter talked me into letting her work for us. I thought about how harsh it would be for Sylvia and her daughter to miss their chance for a green card, and I did not want that guilt trip hanging over my head. I no longer worried that she would kidnap my children. Who in their right mind would kidnap American children and take them to Mexico right after getting a green card? I acquiesced. Sylvia got her green card and once again became a mute fixture in my home, although she continued to work part-time for the other family and lived elsewhere. Now that we'd helped her get her green card, I thought her hatred for me would die away, but I was wrong. I could stand up to any opponent in any courtroom, but our nanny could reduce me to a nervous wreck in my own home. Peter later apologized about his failure to appreciate the depth of my pain around Sylvia. We did plenty of apologizing to each other. But that was later—after our divorce.

❧❧

Sylvia's return to our home was just one of many indicators of Peter's and my dying marriage. Before Leigh turned one year old, it was clear that our marriage was on the rocks and that even our love for our children couldn't bind us together. Each morning, Peter would rise by five o'clock and head into San Francisco, where he often stayed overnight. I would spend time with the kids before heading to my office a few blocks away and pop in and out of the house throughout the day. Sylvia would be there with my little boys and my baby girl.

Increasingly, Peter and I argued over everything, large and small: who was doing more work, who had it harder. We resented each other and seldom spoke about anything other than what needed to be done to keep our train on the tracks. I don't know if kids have a sixth sense, but I was mulling over the state of our marriage when we made a visit to Seattle to see my family. PJ was still a relentless inquisitor, keenly interested in the world, people and relationships. During that visit, PJ accompanied me and my mother to her hair appointment.

While driving across the floating bridge over Lake Washington, my mother and I were chatting away when PJ piped up from the back seat. "Marni," he asked, "Why did you and Papa get divorced?" (My mother had not been keen on being called Grandma, and all of the grandkids called her by her first name.) My eyes widened, but I was too surprised to say anything.

"Oh dear," my mother laughed a bit stiffly. "That was so long ago. I can't remember."

I waited to see if PJ would let it go and tried to remember what my mom and I had just been talking about.

"Did you have a lot of fights?" PJ asked. Oh my God, I thought.

"Oh, I can't remember now," my mom said.

"What was your worst fight?"

"I just can't think."

"Okay, well then just any fight. Can you remember any fight?"

"Not right now. I can't." PJ's line of questioning continued as we pulled off the bridge and drove through the arboretum. I was tongue-tied and didn't know how to get him off his point. Fortunately, we pulled into a parking spot about then and my mom said, "Well, here we are! Time to get my hair done!"

"Will you try to remember a fight with Papa while you're getting your hair done?" PJ asked. PJ and I had a walk and a treat to eat before meeting my freshly coiffed mom an hour later. I had assumed he would forget about Marni and Papa's fights in the meantime—but no sooner had we buckled into the car than PJ asked my mom, "Did you think of any fights while you were getting your hair done?"

"PJ," I said. "We don't want to think about fights." He finally, reluctantly gave up, but he was trying to figure it all out. He wanted to understand why Marni and Papa weren't together anymore. At the same time, I was worried about my own little family, and maybe PJ was, too.

❡17

I know we aren't responsible for our thoughts, let alone our dreams—but shortly before we split, I dreamed that Peter drove our family van off a cliff; my response was to look over the edge and shrug. When I woke up I felt ashamed, even though I knew it was just a dream. All these years later I still remember that dream with sadness and unease.

I had a lot of resentments built up toward the end of our marriage. Not only did I feel displaced by a hostile nanny, I resented what I perceived to be an unfair division of labor. In my head, I was responsible for running the house and supervising the activities of three kids. I worked full time running my own law practice, which was booming. I also managed the family finances and a lot of other things. Blah, blah, blah. To my way of thinking, Peter had it easier because he just worked in his downtown law practice, often staying at fancy hotels in San Francisco rather than coming home to be with me and the kids. Peter and two of his partners (who were also friends of ours) had recently opened the San Francisco office of a large law firm based in Seattle. Their practice was booming, too.

And Peter had started a new entrepreneurial venture developing and presenting meetings around the country on health policy issues, the field he had written his doctoral dissertation on. Peter and I were doing well financially, but we were both exhausted most of the time.

Things were really unraveling by the summer of 1993. My father was not cottoning to being banished by me. "I will not be silenced!" he would declare to my siblings. I picked Linde up at the airport one morning in San Francisco. My father (in his Mr. Hyde persona) had driven her to the airport in Seattle. Linde was deeply upset, saying Dad had told her in the car that I was ruining his life. "I'm going to drive up to the prison in Monroe and get a contract put out on her life." He mentioned a particular killer he planned to visit: the serial killer son of a deceased friend.

Later that day, as I sat at the kitchen table with my head in my hands, Linde commiserating with me, I asked, "What young mother has to worry that her father is going to have her murdered? Why me?" My sister had no answers to the insanity. My siblings were great, but we were all traumatized by our father's behavior; it was all we could do just to be good parents to our own children and keep our heads above water.

These issues did not cause the breakdown of my marriage, but they didn't help things either. Peter had no idea what to do. My dad had always been nice to him, saving his dark side for me. To make matters worse, Peter caught an unfair barrage of my anger and frustration. The frequency of our fights decreased because Peter knew I was buckling under the pressure—but he also stayed away from home more.

One night in the beginning of July, Peter and I lay in bed straight as soldiers all night long, talking about the problems in our marriage. Our sex life was a thing of the distant past, and there was no reviving it. We had tried marriage counseling in good faith for over a year to no avail. That night we talked through our problems, piece by painful piece. I was at the end of my rope, and when Peter told me he loved me that night, I said, "I don't love you." That was the first and only time in our relationship I said such a thing to Peter, and it made him cry. I felt empty, sad and hopeless.

Peter and I got out of bed after a sleepless night, steeling ourselves to face very busy days, as usual. The world marched on, oblivious to our problems. First, PJ and Ben were flying to Texas by themselves to visit Peter's parents, and one of us needed to take them to the airport and get them safely onto the plane. I told Peter it was high time he got involved in such activities and, exhausted and stressed, he called his secretary and told her to cancel all of his meetings for the day. He took the boys to the airport and then headed to his office. Dressed in blue jeans, he dropped by the office just long enough to meet one client before heading back home. Meanwhile, I was preparing to receive a truckload of new furniture. An interior designer was coming along. I had told Peter, "If you want to weigh in on any of this stuff, you'd better be here today." But I was planning to buy whatever I wanted, in hopes that it would make me feel better.

Linde was helping me critique the furnishings and decor coming off the truck. I bounced my baby daughter on my hip and pointed out things I liked. Peter watched for awhile and made a couple of half-hearted suggestions before accepting that his opinion was not welcome. He retreated to the master bedroom to watch television. Not long afterward, he called for me to come quickly to the bedroom. I excused myself from the decorator and movers, handed the baby to Linde, and went to the bedroom to see what Peter was talking about. "Look," he said, pointing to the television. "There's a gunman in downtown San Francisco." We both stared as the camera panned over a familiar street and stopped on One California Street—Peter's office building.

"Oh my God!" I remember saying. "Call your secretary and have her lock the door." Peter's office was on the thirty-second floor in a far corner. Most of the interior offices were separated from the reception area by glass, allowing for sweeping views of San Francisco Bay, but affording no privacy or protection. Peter leapt from the bed and grabbed the phone to warn his secretary and partners of the danger. I will never forget the horror on his face as his secretary sobbed that an intruder had come into their office and shot and killed five people. In a senseless, random rampage that started two stories higher, a lone gunman wandered the halls shooting and killing everyone he could find before finally turning the gun on himself. This heinous crime marked a turning point in my attitude about Peter, our unraveling marriage, and how I would choose to handle my relationship with the father of my children.

❧❦

The day after the shootings, the managing partner of Peter's firm flew with his wife to San Francisco, and I picked them up at the airport. Events were unfolding quickly, and I was nervous when they asked to go to the office. Peter and the managing partner agreed to meet there, and I accompanied them, along with the partner's wife. I was unprepared for the shock of the scene where so many innocent people had died.

Peter's partners described what had happened. They had been working the previous morning, unaware that a gunman harboring an old grudge was shooting and killing people in a law office two stories above them. The shooter made his way down the building's interior staircase before randomly entering Peter's firm's offices. There, the gunman marched past the receptionist and started shooting at people sitting at their desks. People ran for cover and he shot them dead. Some fled; others hid under desks; but ultimately five people in Peter's office were murdered. In each of the offices facing the reception area, the glass panels had been shot out, except for one office in the middle: Peter's. There, the glass was intact and nothing was disturbed on his perfectly orderly desk.

A shiver ran down my spine as I looked at Peter's desk and saw framed photographs of me and the kids smiling out over the horrific scene. At that moment, the realization hit me with full force that if Peter had been in the office the previous morning, he surely would have been killed. My knees nearly buckled. In fifteen years I had never known Peter to cancel a meeting. That was one of my major gripes—he was always in the office. Peter later told me that three other people were supposed to be in a conference with him in his office that morning. All of them were spared because he cancelled the meeting.

Four souls survived because of our failing marriage and sleepless night.

In the following weeks, as Peter and I went to funerals and pressed forward, we clung to each other for comfort. His voice sounded like music to me. I thought of my crazy dream in which I shrugged after he drove off a cliff, and was awash with relief that my true feelings were nothing like that. Just watching Peter breathe was magical. Everything moved in slow motion. My heart ached for those who were killed and the families who lost loved ones. I kept pinching myself at our strange fate. My children did not lose their father to a savage and senseless murder. I did not lose my husband after telling him for the first and only time that I did not love him. I had the opportunity—and have taken it many times—to tell Peter what a wonderful person and father he is.

After Peter's close brush, I think we both thought we could overcome all our troubles. But as the weeks slipped by, the problems in our relationship resurfaced, and we were right back to the same place, living separate lives. Still, I will never forget that day or the lesson I learned: Relationships—even marriages—can come and go, wax and wane, flame up and sputter out. But life is precious and, no matter how mad I was at Peter, I was thankful beyond belief that he was still alive—and that our faltering marriage hadn't been the victim of such a cruel and brutal end.

❡18

After the tragedy in Peter's office, I felt a deep sense of hopelessness. I was profoundly grateful Peter had survived when others had so senselessly died, and I felt guilty thinking about my own problems in the face of such tragedy. But I could not beat my depression. As my self-esteem sank, I told my sister that I felt like a squashed bug.

"What?" Linde cried out in alarm. "How can you say that? You are a wonderful, pretty woman, a great mom and a fantastic lawyer! I can't stand to hear you say such a thing about yourself."

"But it's true," I said. "I've lost myself. It's as if I'm made of vapor and you could wave a wand right through me without touching anything."

"Gail," my sister said. "This is not okay. You have always been brave and strong. You have to get back in touch with yourself and feel good again." I knew she was right.

I talked with Amy, who also bolstered me. "I've gone through times in my life where I felt like that too," she said. "You need to find your center."

I spent hours visiting with Amy while our children romped and played around our houses. As was our penchant, Amy and I revisited issues from our childhoods and talked about how these experiences had shaped the rest of our lives. Amy's parents had also divorced when she was young. We are both the youngest of three sisters (although she doesn't have a younger sibling, as I do). We related on so many levels. We laughed a lot, making fun of ourselves and teasing each other. Amy loved to call me Miss Thang. I was always juggling ten different things and, in the early 1990s, had way too many plates in the air. Amy made me feel happier and helped me bring my problems "down to size." But, she also wisely encouraged me to work through my issues with my therapist.

As I struggled with the loneliness in my marriage and the feeling that I was made of vapor, I wondered where I had lost myself along the way. Despite my parents' divorce, I remembered having confidence as a child: I had been a capable student, finding it easy to make good grades; I had enjoyed singing and playing the guitar; I had been an excellent horseback rider and loved my horse, Sytan. In therapy, I explored difficult childhood issues that carried over into my adult life. During this time, Peter wanted nothing to do with individual therapy, but he did participate in marital counseling. I resented the feeling I sometimes got from Peter that because I was the one in therapy, there was something wrong with me. I believed it took courage to face demons—therapy wasn't always easy, but I learned a lot along the way.

Thoughts of divorce began to percolate again in my consciousness, and I raised the issue with Amy from time to time.

I saw what she had with Roy, and I longed for a similar deep, intimate connection with a man. I knew Peter and I could never get there, no matter how much we both might want to.

"I want a new beginning, but I can't stand the thought of a bitter divorce," I once said to Amy. And she said something that surprised me.

"Gail, you and Peter are in many ways already divorced. You lead separate lives and are essentially divorced within your marriage." She was, of course, right. Like so many others who function as a married couple on many levels (sharing a home, finances and children), Peter and I had never attained an intimate bond; we were ships passing in the night. Amy then said something else that intrigued me. "If it comes to that, I think you and Peter are capable of having a good divorce."

"What do you mean?" I asked.

"Well, you're both really good people. Maybe you're just not a good match. You both adore your children. You like and respect each other. I think you have the capacity to handle a divorce well."

I had never really considered the concept of a good divorce. But I couldn't face the prospect of being this unhappy and lonely for the rest of my life. I lay in bed alone at night thinking. Could Peter and I have a good divorce? I shuddered at the thought. But over and again, I started to ask myself questions: What would happen if we got divorced? Would the kids be okay? Would Peter and I be okay? What might our lives look like? Could I find happiness with someone else downstream? The questions were overwhelming, but they kept coming. Could we possibly have a good divorce?

❧19

After the shooting that took the lives of friends, Peter and I both looked deeply inward. I'm the one who loves to write, but Peter wrote me some long, thoughtful letters during the prelude to our separation. Those letters are deeply personal, but with his permission I share with you something he wrote and acted upon after our divorce:

> *We stand at a crossroads requiring decisions*
> *fundamental to our one life on earth and all those*
> *we love. . . . In recent weeks we have been brutalized*
> *by one of the most violent acts conceivable—and*
> *you have been wonderful in your sincere and loving*
> *support —and we have worked until we are almost*
> *physically ill. I truly believe that we are each doing*
> *the best that we can. In the ashes I feel a strong*
> *sense of rebirth. We can change our lives. Life is*
> *not really lived without intensity, without risk,*
> *without pain and joy. I love you and I love our family.*
> *Whatever happens, I will act on that love.*

I cannot begin to describe my gratitude at having had the opportunity to hear Peter tell me he loved me and to be able to tell him—truthfully—that I loved him, too. As I've said, we tried hard after the tragedy to rekindle our marriage. We did love each other. But too much water had passed under the bridge in our personal relationship. Our marriage was over. It was irretrievably broken and could not be revived. Yet we had a long history together, and neither of us wanted to vilify the other. More importantly, our futures were inextricably linked by the children we loved.

❧❧

Peter and I decided to separate before we finalized our divorce. We agreed that I would stay in the house with the children and he would get his own place. Peter and I hadn't fought over money too much in the past. Our problems didn't involve the lack of money, but rather the fact that, often, we wanted to spend it (or not) on different things. Peter valued travel; I wanted a beautiful home. He liked to treat friends to great seats at the Super Bowl; I didn't like football. I wanted to move to a different house; he didn't want a different house. During our marriage we ran along at breakneck pace, sometimes like clumsy partners in a potato sack race. We hired an accountant to help us make budgets, but we could never stick to them. Although far from the breaking point, money was a source of frustration from time to time and one more thing we couldn't seem to manage well together.

When we were separating, our accountant reminded us that legal bills for divorces often wipe out the divorcing couple's finances. He suggested we reach an agreement ourselves if we could. Because we were both lawyers, we decided to give it a try. We hired a no-nonsense family-law attorney to help us cut a financial deal. It didn't take us long to divide up what we had. In the end we had a pretty even fifty/fifty split.

I don't suggest non-lawyers should represent themselves, even if they are cooperating. In fact, years later, Peter and I had to revisit the issue of money, and we needed attorneys to help us understand our rights and obligations. Contrary to popular perception, good attorneys, such as the ones who helped us, understand the value of preserving the good will between parents, and work hard to achieve a fair and peaceful resolution. But given our stormy (and sometimes petty) history, I have always been proud that Peter and I did not fight over money and stuff when we split. We figured—correctly—that it was a zero-sum game.

If any good can come of evil, the tragedy Peter and I experienced before our break-up loosened our grip on possessions, money and the need to always be right. After we reached our agreement, Peter gave me some praise and recognition that I longed to hear. I thanked him for things he did, too. Thanking each other for our efforts marked a new beginning of cooperation for us. There might be a limit to the amount of gratitude couples can show each other as they go through a divorce, but in reflecting upon the success of our divorce, it all boils down to the fact that, over time, Peter and I simply forgave each other and ourselves.

❧20

In the early days of our divorce, the pain was so raw it was hard even to get out of bed. Interacting with each other was trying, to say the least. But sometimes we had to work together for the good of the children—no matter what. One such occasion was breaking the news to our children about our plans to separate. Peter and I agreed that we would tell the kids together. PJ was nine and Ben was seven; Leigh was just a year and a half.

On the day we sat down to talk to the kids, Peter and I were both scared and sad. We sat at the sunny eating booth in the breakfast room of our Mill Valley house, the same table where I had placed Ben's baby seat when we came home from the hospital. Peter and I spoke to the boys with forced cheer in our voices. I put Leigh in her high chair where she happily banged her fist and kept up a steady stream of baby banter.

PJ glowed happily as we settled down into our seats. "These are my favorite times in the world," he announced. "I just love it when we're all together like this."

I kept a small smile pasted on my face, but my heart broke. In the pregnant moment before having to break this difficult news, the only thing that helped me was seeing the corner of the townhouse Peter had bought behind our neighbor's yard. In that moment, I put aside my selfish desire for space and clung to the hope that having two households in close proximity would soften the blow. Even so, it was very, very sad.

I don't recall the words—so many years later, it still hurts to think of that day. But I desperately wanted to do it right. Peter and I had planned when and how we would tell our children. We pulled together and explained that, even though we loved each other and adored all three of our children, we had decided we needed to live apart. You can imagine the string of questions that burst forth from PJ. He asked if we were getting divorced, and we said that we were. "Do we have to go to church for that?" he asked with alarm. No, we assured him, we did not have to go to church. Ben, as usual, soaked in the information more quietly. Soon, though, we were all walking to Peter's townhouse and talking about all the cool things they would have there, like bunk beds and a life-size cardboard cutout of Michael Jordan in the living room!

It was very, very hard when Peter moved out. Despite our efforts to cooperate for the kids, we were upset, raw, and angry—in short, we had the full range of emotions divorcing couples typically experience. We did not skip any of these normal emotions, but we worked hard to manage them instead of letting them manage us.

While all of this was going on, I was trying to make peace with my dad. I'd had a conference call with him and all my siblings. By then, I hadn't seen him in five years. I took the reins and said I would resume seeing him on the condition he observed the boundaries: no talk *ever* about sex, religion or my mother. It was a "take it or leave it" offer. Reluctantly, he agreed.

In the first rocky days after our separation, Peter showed up at the front door and knocked. That in itself felt bizarre. There was a brass lion knocker on the front door that Peter, I doubt, had ever noticed before. Now, here he was tapping it politely in order to gain admittance to the house. I opened the door and our conversation went something like this:

"Hi."

"Hi."

I cleared my throat. "How are you?"

"Fine," Peter answered. We both felt awkward and stood for a moment in silence. "I bought a book on etiquette to read while we're getting used to this," he said.

I almost fell over. "Etiquette?"

"I thought it might help." Then, as if on cue from Emily Post, he asked, "May I come in, please?"

I felt like a player in the theater of the absurd as I stepped back and made some comment like, "Do come in." We were too raw to make small talk, but I sent the kids off with him and, in just about that way, we got through our earliest exchanges of kids without problems. It hurt—of course it did. My feelings of awkwardness and grief surged when Peter appeared at our doorstep and rang the bell as a stranger. I needed time to process this, but it would have to wait until the children had left the house. For the time being, the priority was for our children to see both their parents making a sincere effort to adjust, and to see that we did it with kindness—and maybe even a sense of humor.

One of the weird and painful realizations I had immediately after the separation was that Peter started seeing the kids a lot more than when we had been together. One of my frustrations in the marriage was that he was gone all the time, getting up at six in the morning and leaving for the office, even on the weekends. I had been so lonely. And the boys had often asked me when they were going to see their dad. "When is Dad going to be home?" they'd ask as we were driving in the car.

"Pretty soon," I would say, because I didn't know when he would be back. But after we separated, Peter did an about-face. He turned his condo into a virtual playground. I struggled with questions like, "Hey, what's wrong with me? Now that I'm out of the picture, he wants to spend a lot of time with the kids." But I told myself to let it go, because the boys were spending time with their dad. Lots of it. Leigh was still little—just a year and a half—and Peter was not comfortable keeping her for long stretches yet. This meant that I had lots of time alone with her: dressing her, playing games with her, combing her fabulous long curls. I cherished that time.

Peter continued to employ Sylvia at his condo. She was devoted to him, but she was prim, polite and judgmental with me. Peter still believed Sylvia was the glue that kept things on track. I had long since given up the struggle to make my point, let alone to get her out of my life.

Without mentioning the etiquette book again, Peter kept treating me politely, and I treated him the same way. This was in the days before e-mail, and we often relied on the telephone and voice mails to communicate. We kept it short and polite. When our nerves were jangled or we said or heard something that set off old triggers, we both bit our tongues. It's amazing we didn't permanently damage our tongues as we bit them instead of wagged them! But it paid off. Some things are better left unsaid.

❧21

Divorce lawyers and counselors will tell you that one of the things that helps most in building a cooperative co-parenting relationship with your ex is to live close to each other. I've known others who have made it work from across the country, but proximity was key in Peter's and my experience.

When Peter and I split up, he decided to purchase one of the new townhouses being built on a parcel just a block away from our family house. With a good arm, you could throw a rock from my house and hit the one Peter bought. I was angry, thinking he intended to monitor me, but I said nothing. If Peter decided to buy my whole block, there was nothing I could do about it. Peter later commented that he could not only see my front gate but hear it shut from his back deck. He said it comforted him, and the kids absolutely loved having him so close by.

It was more than strange to be sitting on my back porch during those first evenings on my own, hearing my kids' happy voices whooping away over at Peter's. As I said, he set his place up as a giant playground. While I busied myself decorating my house with grown-up furnishings, Peter erected the Michael

Jordan cutout in the corner of his living room and placed a basketball hoop nearby. Michael Jordan smiled over the boys as they stuffed basketballs in the hoop. When Leigh was at Peter's, she loved to scoot on her bottom down the two stories of carpeted stairs, shouting as her bottom bumped along the steps. It was pandemonium over there and, as I sat at my house sipping a glass of wine in those early days, I had mixed emotions. Part of me was feeling sorry for myself, missing all that fun. Another part of me thought, thank God I am not trapped in that loony bin. I walked through the peaceful rooms of my house listening to beautiful music and told myself it was okay. Everybody's okay. It's not perfect—but it's okay.

❧❧❧

In the last years of my marriage and after our separation, I became extremely close to Amy and Roy. We especially loved Friday nights. At five o'clock on the dot, Roy, who was a music lover and a great disc jockey, would put on some music and crank up the volume. The lead-off tune was usually, "*You Drive Me Crazy*" by the Fine Young Cannibals. Our front doors were always wide open to accommodate the back-and-forth traffic of the boys, and when the first beats of that music blared, we dropped everything and made a beeline for Roy and Amy's living room. We all danced. The boys did the Gator, and we clapped and laughed and kicked off the weekend.

I've never been a great dancer, but I loved to do my thing anyway and especially loved watching Amy and Roy dance together. Amy had been in stage productions of *Hair* and *Jesus Christ Superstar* and was a fabulous dancer. Roy spun her around, and her long red hair flew as the boys sprang around the floor, whooping and Gatoring. Leigh screamed with joy, clapped her hands and stamped her little feet. No wonder dance is one of Leigh's passions, and that Ben has become a great party DJ. In the years after our divorce, Peter has deepened his relationship with Amy and Roy—but in those days, they were my soul mates.

Amy, Roy and I formed a reading club called Los Treblos (a nonsensical phrase meaning The Three) and took turns selecting books to read and discuss over long dinners and glasses of wine while the kids played. Amy and I picked "reasonable" books like *Bird by Bird*, while Roy tortured us with heavy-duty tomes like *A Light in August* and *Sometimes a Great Notion*. Amy and I fancied ourselves intellectuals and were not about to give up on those books, but we'd grumble with each other, saying, "What page are *you* on?" "How are you coming along with *Sometimes a Vague Notion*?" We fixed wonderful dinners and exchanged many *totally intellectual* ideas after we'd finished those damn books.

Yes, friends and family helped us through the transition. Peter's mom, whom I adore, was deeply upset and worried for the children when we split. And as a good, loyal mom, she was pretty mad at me for awhile. Divorce ripples out to affect all of the ones we love. But Peter's mom came around. She knew what I had gone through with my dad and had witnessed my anguish. She is a loving woman, and we reestablished—and cherish—a caring bond. (I spent a week with her in Texas last year. We lolled back in our easy chairs, ate Frango Mints from Seattle, watched *International House Hunters* for hours, and told each other which houses we'd pick. It took awhile for both of us to get there, but the passage of time works wonders if only we're willing to forgive and forget.)

❧22

The first Christmas after our separation, my mom came down to visit. I was thinking of moving to a different house in Mill Valley, and after working for awhile on Christmas dinner preparations, I took her on a drive to see a house I was considering. The kids were at Peter's, so we took our time, and stopped by the store an hour or so after we'd left home. As we stood in line, I started thinking about a pan I had put on the stove.

I turned to my mom. "Did you happen to turn off the simmering giblets?"

"No," she said, alarm registering in her eyes. "Didn't you?"

"*Oh no,*" I said. In one motion, my mother and I abandoned our grocery cart and raced for the door.

"There was only about a cup of water in that pan," I said, as we sped toward the house.

"The liquid is long gone," my mom said. "We've been gone for an hour and a half!"

As we turned onto our street, I could see fire engines in front of the house. Smoke billowed from the front door and a swarm of firefighters filled the front yard and street. As I pulled up and stopped the car, I could see there were no flames, but a huge fan was filling the open front door. I climbed out of the car and looked toward Amy's yard, where she was standing with a video camera on her shoulder.

"Miss Thang cooks a turkey," she said with a laugh.

All's well that ends well (this has become a motto of mine). So I burned up a pan of giblets. Oh well. The firefighters were cute and very nice about it. But I still hate to cook turkey.

෴

There is no doubt about it: divorce is hard on one's self-esteem, even when both spouses work hard to avoid confrontation and recriminations. It's impossible not to wonder what went wrong. I asked myself, "Could I have done things differently? Will I ever be happy again?" For a long time, I was exhausted physically and emotionally. At the end of every busy, crazy work day, I'd end up in bed alone, listening to music. I loved wistful, romantic songs that seemed to capture my loneliness and longing for someone to hold and love. In those quiet hours, I began letting myself imagine having someone in my life to love and to cherish, to have and to hold. I wasn't thinking about marriage vows. I was dreaming about merging souls and, yes, bodies. How I yearned for a deep, intimate connection with a man.

One night as I listened to the music in the dark, I looked through the skylight I'd had installed above my bed so I could look at the night sky. The stars were sparkling in the distance. I'd been so bogged down in my problems and challenges that

I'd forgotten to trust and hope for my future. I was proving that I could survive on my own, and I knew I did not need a man to be whole. I'd lie in bed thinking, "Is it possible I'll ever be able to find love again?" (I was well over thirty and feeling pretty old.) But still I wondered. "Is there someone out there for me? If he is out there somewhere, what is he doing? Is he looking at these same stars and wondering if he'll ever find love again?"

I looked at the stars, knowing I shouldn't look for a man to solve all my problems, but desperately wanting love. I allowed myself a prayer, just in case. "Wherever you may be, my darling, I'm sending my love to you tonight. I hope we will find each other someday."

❧23

When Peter and I split up our household, my primary client was still embroiled in litigation, and I continued traveling back and forth across the country. Peter and I cooperated on caring for the kids when we traveled. Failure to do so would have been pointless, petty and expensive. I was working with lawyers in Michigan, New York and Washington D.C., and in those days before e-mail became the norm, my fax machine and copiers hummed all day long. But one day, as the number of lawsuits and costs of litigation spiraled skyward, my client filed for Chapter 11 bankruptcy protection, and everything came to a screeching halt. All of the law firms received notification to stop working until further notice. My client informed me they would be asking the federal court in Michigan to approve me as special counsel in the bankruptcy case, but they had never been through the process, and neither had I. Everyone was feeling their way.

I had a fantastic group of attorneys and paralegals working with me, and I was deeply saddened that the loss of work forced me to let them go. Fortunately, they were all able to land on their feet. But as I sat alone in that quiet office, I suddenly felt fear—and the urge to move home to Seattle. I was at loose ends after the divorce and in the midst of huge professional change. I wanted my kids to know their cousins. I had reached détente with my dad, and I was drawn back to my roots. I soon went to Peter and begged him to consider relocating to Seattle.

"Your law firm is based there," I argued. He looked at me like I'd lost my mind.

"I don't have any business in Seattle," he responded.

"Your business is all over the country! You'll love it. Please, Peter, think about it." I had no leverage at all. Under California law as it existed at the time, Peter could have prevented me from taking the kids out of the state. Either my wheedling or persuasive skills paid off, because soon Peter and I were on a plane to Seattle. In a previous trip, I had already located a house I wanted to buy in a family-oriented neighborhood that had several other possible properties nearby. I buried my nose in a magazine as Peter scowled at a book. I didn't dare nag him because I had him on a plane heading to Seattle! The real estate agent picked us up, and I showed Peter the house I wanted. He eyed the swimming pool in the backyard.

"I don't want Leigh being near a pool. She can't swim," he said. "Maybe you could fill it with sand."

"Yeah, maybe I could," I said.

After looking at a couple of blah houses, we walked into one that had been owned by a single dad. It had a profession-al-looking basketball court in the backyard. Peter took one look at that basketball court, did a quick swing through the house to count the bedrooms, and turned on his heel to walk back to the agent's car as I trotted along behind. Without any further ado, he said to me, "I won't do anything to pull off this move because I'm too busy. But if you handle the move, I guess I'll go ahead and do it. But Sylvia will have to come with us." I didn't grovel at his feet in gratitude, but I wanted to. I didn't even freak out over Sylvia coming along. What an act of grace he showed me that day.

Some people thought at the time that Peter should have exercised his power to hold me down while he could. He could have forced me to suffer the loss of my income and to move to a less expensive suburb while he maintained a home in Mill Valley. He could have marginalized me and gloated over his victory. But here is what happened: Peter knew I needed my family and wanted my kids to know their cousins. And his business really wasn't based in San Francisco; it was all over the country. He decided to take the high road, and our family is better and stronger for it.

Readers of early drafts of this book asked me for a deeper explanation of why Peter cooperated with me when he had the power to hold me down. I know that his love for our children was his driving motivation. But I think Peter chose to cooperate with me because we had loved each other when we married and had children. We'd always respected each other. We both worked hard to be good to each other and our kids. Peter knew we'd made mistakes, but that we were both fundamentally good human beings. Peter is a loving man. He's not gushingly emotive, but he is loyal. He's excitable, but not mean. He is able to bounce back from criticism. He deeply loves his children and wants their mother to be okay. He forgave me for my failings and forgave himself for his own failings. He appreciated my efforts to get along with him and understood that life would go more smoothly for all of us if we buried the hatchet and moved on. One can never read another person's mind, but this is what I believe about Peter's treatment of me after our divorce.

I also believe Peter got a peace dividend for moving to Seattle after our divorce, because he got a fresh start that he didn't anticipate. Those days after the shooting in San Francisco were heartrending. Peter's firm moved to a new location, and the surviving employees slowly pulled themselves together. Peter was close to all of those people. He kept his office in San Francisco for years, but he liked Seattle from the start. He liked his house, bought a boat with friends, and ultimately met and married a woman he would never have known if he hadn't moved as an accommodation to me—his ex-wife.

¶24

One of the harsh realities of divorce is that when a marriage goes by the boards, friendships that centered around the marriage can go with it. I saw my mother suffer after her divorce as lifelong friends excluded her from dinner parties and other social events. A divorced person can feel like a pariah as married couples seem to close ranks and leave newly single friends behind. Married people in unhappy unions sometimes fear that divorce is contagious. And in some ways, it is. Once one couple in a social circle splits up, others in the group may ask themselves, "Am I happy in my marriage? Do I have options?" Other couples don't judge their divorced friends unkindly. They simply don't know how to adjust to the changed dynamic. And sometimes, perhaps without realizing it, divorced people can become pains in the neck, complaining, ranting and raving about their exes long after their friends have grown weary of the narrative. Instead of holding up their hands and saying, "Enough! I've heard all of this already," the friends stop calling. Most of us know at least one person who has never tired of burdening everyone with horror stories about their ex.

But sometimes in our lives, we are given the gift of meeting someone who becomes a deep and enduring friend—someone who doesn't judge others. I had found such a friend in Amy.

As the day approached for me to move to Seattle, Amy and I went for lunch to a favorite, cozy Italian restaurant in Corte Madera and, over the span of four hours, we ate a cup of soup and drank a bottle of wine while we sobbed and told each other how much we loved and would miss each other. I presumptuously told Roy once that I loved Amy as much as he did. I must have lost my mind to say such a thing, but Roy handled it with one of his beautiful smiles. He could hardly blame anyone for loving Amy. After God made Amy, he broke the mold.

❡25

In August 1995, we moved to Seattle. I had taken the Washington Bar Exam in July and was waiting for the results. My client had applied to the federal court in Michigan to have me appointed as special bankruptcy counsel, and I was awaiting that decision as well. I had placed my Mill Valley house on the market and had purchased the house in Washington. In short, I had two houses to pay for, no job and no license to practice in Washington.

Amy and Roy cooked wonderful dinners for me every night for the last week or two before I left California. My dad, relieved to be back in the fold and eager to be helpful, flew down to drive my station wagon with our two dogs to Seattle. Peter drove his car with the two boys so they could stop at scenic places along the route. Leigh and I would fly up after I closed down the house. I held Leigh on my hip, and we waved with Amy and Roy as the two cars carrying Peter, the boys, my dad and our dogs started together down Mountain View Avenue. Amy and I wept as Travis and Jesse ran down the street after them, waving and screaming good bye. We knew that the boys, who are now men, would preserve their friendships (helped by periodic visits between our families), but at the time there was no question that a beautiful era was ending.

When Peter moved to Seattle, my family pulled out the stops to help him in the transition and to show gratitude for his gracious act. My brother-in-law, a general contractor, and his partner did extensive renovations on both houses before we made the move. The houses looked great. Peter and I had no disagreements over the logistics, but had some prickly conversations about the swimming pool in my backyard. I, too, was paranoid about having a pool when Leigh did not yet know how to swim. But the pool had an automatic cover that opened and closed with an electrical switch, and I promised to open it only when the kids were being directly supervised. I couldn't blame Peter for being nervous when I wouldn't even let Leigh eat lollypops in the car for fear she could be injured in an accident. We worked through the issue, and Leigh, of course, learned to swim like a fish.

But in the early days after our move, our wildly different lifestyles became more pronounced. Peter and I were no longer unwilling partners in a potato sack race. We each got to create our own households. We now lived blocks apart in a large neighborhood. The kids quickly made lots of friends, and we accumulated a fleet of bicycles that the kids used to flow back and forth between our houses and their many friends' homes.

Our different styles were reflected in the way we set up our homes. Peter filled his living room with a drum set, piano and a vast assortment of video games. His family room decor consisted of a life-sized stuffed gorilla surrounded by a couple dozen other stuffed animals, a leather couch and a big-screen TV. He had hundreds of movies and loved watching them with the kids. I, on the other hand, had the usual assortment of furnishings and, for the lack of a better term, a "grown-up" house. I found the disparity between household styles to be quite challenging at times because the playhouse nature of Peter's place had a magnetic draw for the kids.

In some ways, Peter is like a big kid. He loves constant activity, followed by a nap. Alice once affectionately said of him, "Peter is not a human being—he's a human event!" As soon as we moved to Seattle, Peter bought season's tickets to the Seattle Sonics basketball games and immediately started taking the boys to each and every home game. The boys were in fifth and third grades and were sometimes going to as many as three games per week, some of them on weeknights. I wasn't keen on this idea, but was not about to start criticizing Peter, who was enthusiastically embracing Seattle's sports teams with the boys. Peter had purchased an extra ticket and would often take a friend along. I would hear about the evenings' excitement after the fact.

"I got my arm stuck in the cup holder on my seat," PJ said one morning after the game.

"Yeah, the paramedics had to come cut him out," Ben said, while munching on his toast.

A guy affectionately called "Tuba Man" by Seattle basketball fans played his tuba outside Key Arena, and people tossed bills in his tuba case as they walked to the games. One night after Peter and the kids had gone to the game, PJ called me from a pay phone at the sports arena: "Mom," he whispered into the phone. "Dad gave our extra ticket to Tuba Man, and he's sitting with us. He smells really bad and he's screaming a lot. What should I do?"

Thinking on the fly, I came up with the best advice I could muster. "Nothing, darling. Just enjoy the game and let Tuba Man enjoy it, too."

Not too long after that, PJ told me at breakfast, "I got my arm stuck in the cup holder on my chair and the paramedics had to come."

"I know, honey. You told me that a couple weeks ago."

"It happened again," Ben said, munching his toast.

Even though I found it hard to compete with Peter's activities with the kids—I didn't gravitate to those things myself—I tried to go with the flow.

❡26

Sylvia was originally enthusiastic about moving to Seattle, but after moving with her daughter into a condominium near our neighborhood, she became unhappy. She and her daughter missed Mill Valley. When Sylvia was at my house, she seldom uttered a word to me, and she was becoming uncharacteristically frazzled by the boys' bickering. They were arguing a lot in elementary school, and this required constant refereeing and the patience of Job. One day, Sylvia asked if she could speak with me. We sat down in the living room, and she told me she quit. I sat there and blinked in disbelief before asking her what had happened. She told me the boys had been fighting and she couldn't take it anymore. She said she'd come back the next day, but that was it. I could hardly believe she was serious, but she seemed in earnest.

The next day, Peter came to my house at the end of the day. The three of us sat down together in my living room. Peter clearly did not believe Sylvia was quitting either. He was prepared to smooth over one more rough patch. But Sylvia had already told PJ and Ben earlier that day that she was quitting because they wouldn't stop fighting with each other. They had run to me with popping eyes and questions, and were waiting in their rooms while the grown-ups had this big confab. I was furious that after ten years, Sylvia would blame the boys for her sudden departure, leaving them to feel they had done something seriously wrong. All they'd been doing was walloping each other with their lunch pails and calling each other names—standard little boy behavior. At that meeting in my living room, I sat quietly while Peter told Sylvia he understood she was tired and needed a rest. He said we could hire someone to fill in for her until she felt better.

Sylvia said, "You don't understand. I quit."

I said, "Well, goodbye. Do you want me to call a taxi?"

"No," she said. She stood up and walked out the door.

I felt like the sun had just risen after an ice age. I had for so long wanted this woman, with her sullen moods and thinly veiled hatred, out of my life. But I was worried about the effect her abrupt departure might have on the children, who didn't understand what had happened. The next day, I hired a babysitter through an agency. She was a cheerful, lovely woman who, as it turned out, would work for us for years. I never had a flicker of a bad feeling with her. But issues surrounding Sylvia raised painful questions of loyalty long after she was physically gone. I did not understand how members of my own family could continue a relationship with someone who had caused me such grief. Lingering fears that she had stolen some part of my children's affections haunted me. I could never get Peter to feel my pain, let alone give me the solace and validation I felt I deserved. He did apologize years later for not supporting me on this. The apology assuaged my hurt, but it came long after Sylvia was gone.

❡27

The question of loyalty inevitably plays out in any divorce, often forcing family members and friends to make difficult choices. My parents both wanted validation after divorce and sought support from their children. We kids were stuck in the middle. My father's way of making himself feel better was often to vilify my mother behind her back. But when parents behave like enemies and criticize their ex in this way, their children inevitably feel guilty, helpless, disloyal and stained. It is also painful when friends choose sides, either overtly or subtly, and once-close relationships wither away. Even friends who do not harshly judge divorce may want a balanced dinner table or struggle with which ex to invite. As my mother once said when feeling blue, "The world goes by in twos." Being divorced can be lonely.

In my lonely times, I turned to spiritual readings and was amazed to discover the most unusual, erotic and emotional love poem in, of all places, the Bible. The "*Song of Songs*," or "*Solomon's Song*," as translated by Eugene Peterson in *The Message*, tells a love story that takes place between a man and woman in biblical times. The woman is no adolescent Juliet, but rather the embodiment of mature, feminine, earthly love. The man and woman speak passionately to each other of their love for one another and, implicitly, of God. The woman, knowing she no longer possesses the full bloom of youth, tells her lover:

> *I am weathered but still elegant,*
> *oh, dear sisters in Jerusalem,*
> *Weather-darkened like Kedar desert tents,*
> *time-softened like Solomon's Temple hangings.*
> *Don't look down on me because I'm dark,*
> *darkened by the sun's harsh rays.*
> *My brothers ridiculed me and sent me to*
> *work in the fields.*
> *They made me care for the face of the earth,*
> *but I had no time to care for my own face.*

Weathered but still elegant! That was how *I* wanted to feel. I was forty years old and single. My father had rejected my mother when she was forty, and had repeatedly told me and my sisters that women are undesirable after the age of thirty. I longed to feel beautiful and lovable, and resisted believing my chances of being passionately desired and cherished by a man were gone. I read and re-read the "Song of Songs," marveling that such a love poem had been included in the Bible.

❧❧

In these lonely moments, it was especially hard to have Peter roll into the driveway to pick up the children and then head off on some grand adventure or even an ordinary family outing—minus mom. But I made myself smile and wave as they drove away. "Move over Meryl Streep," I'd think as I shut the door and sagged against it. "*You* may be winning the Academy Award again this year, but I feel I deserve it for that performance."

Other times, I must confess, that silence was golden. As the car pulled out of the driveway, I could open a good book, call my sister, go to a movie, have a personal life. It's true—absence makes the heart grow fonder. On one of the days my kids were off having fun with Peter, I told my brother, Bob, that as long as my kids were okay, I was going to be okay. "A good divorce can be pretty darned nice," I said. "I feel happy now, and I just hope and pray my children are as happy as they seem."

"You and Peter both seem happy. And happy people raise happy children," he said. "Married or not."

❡28

Looking back, I think of my first Seattle home with warm amusement. Chaos often reigned. My attorney friend, Carolyn, who'd worked with me in Mill Valley, flew up to help me with legal work in Seattle. She cracked up one day as I ran through the house corralling the kids and yelling at them to get into some decent clothes. I had forgotten we had a professional photograph session scheduled and had about twenty minutes to get there. The kids were used to this kind of chaos and good naturedly put on the clothes I grabbed for them, but we couldn't find anyone's shoes. I dressed Leigh in a beautiful dress her grandmother had hand-sewn and strapped her into her car seat wearing that dress and some grubby tennis shoes. When we traipsed into the photography studio, I quickly brushed Leigh's waist-length curls, and all three kids posed with lovely smiles in a waist-up shot that still has a treasured place in my heart and home. Only I know that beneath the handsome shirts and lovely dress were frayed jeans and grungy tennis shoes. And the cascade of beautiful hair tumbling to Leigh's waist never looked so perfect again—she took the scissors to her hair a couple days later and cut off a chunk of curls at her hairline.

I have never understood how people can make their kids keep clean bedrooms in one home—let alone two. I gave up trying at my house. I just shut their bedroom doors and treated them as outlying areas that didn't really count. Every six months or so, though, I enjoyed helping the kids clean their rooms. We'd haul a huge garbage sack upstairs and start off by filling it up with old school papers, broken stuff and whatever else needed to be tossed. We'd scrounge around under their beds and bust through their closets. We'd finish off by polishing their nightstands with furniture polish so everything gleamed. Then we'd make their beds and—just for that one night—we'd stand back and gloat with satisfaction. I did ask my kids to make their beds lots of other times, and they said they'd do it. But they rarely did. Instead, they'd shout, as the door banged shut behind them, "I'm going to Dad's! See you later!" I could have run after them and forced them to tidy up before they left, but I just let it go. Gradually their bedrooms slipped into chaos until we had another deep-cleaning session some six months later. And later still, I sent them off into the world to be forced by headmasters or roommates to perform this simple task on a regular basis. Or not.

But the rest of the house was another matter. My sister, Linde, referred us to her house cleaner, a delightful gay guy named Dave. Dave could clean a house like nobody's business, but his nerves were already frayed from cleaning my sister's house, not to mention my dad's. Linde is the most organized person I know, but her husband could eat popcorn by the barrelful and leave trails of it all over the floor. It nearly drove Dave (and Linde) mad. And my dad had a lovely house with a fabulous garden, but cleaning his house would have made anyone insane. When Dave added my house and Peter's to his roster, he really teetered on the brink. But he used to crack so many jokes that I totally adored him, and I believe he really liked us—although he eventually moved to Florida and never came back.

Dave came to a party at my house once, and I overheard him telling someone: "The family is driving me insane. And I don't mean my own." Ah, come on, Dave, the truth is that it's really hard to make your kids clean their rooms when you raise them in two households. It's too easy for them to escape back and forth, and to time their messes around the cleaning crew.

"Didn't I just pick these damn shoes off the floor at your dad's house?" I'd hear Dave bellow toward the swimming pool.

"What? What? I can't hear you!" The kids would holler as they cannonballed into the water. Good old Dave. We all really miss him.

❡29

For awhile after we moved to Washington, things went so smoothly between us that I began to wonder whether Peter and I had made a big mistake getting divorced. Here we had these three fabulous kids we both adored, and we were getting along without fighting! And Sylvia was gone! Maybe things weren't perfect, but they seemed pretty darned good.

Peter and I began talking with a family counselor about ways to discipline our boys in a coordinated way. If I was secretly glad the boys had bickered Sylvia out of my life, I grudgingly had to admit it was pretty irksome to deal with the fracas. Peter and I explained to the counselor that they quarreled a lot and always wanted us to choose sides and mediate things. The counselor spoke to all four of us together and then spoke with the boys alone, and then with just Peter and me. She was ready to give us the answer to our dilemma. We sat with bated breath as she looked at us and smiled.

"Your boys are fine," she said. We sighed, relieved, and waited for her to continue. She smiled again and said, "The problem is you."

Peter and I blinked and exchanged glances. "Us?"

"Yes," she said matter-of-factly. "You." The gist of her opinion, which was not unkind, was that we needed to accept that our kids were going to bicker.

"You mean to say we have to listen to all of this bickering and sort through it?" I asked. "We have to figure out who did what and try to resolve it?"

"Yes. That's what parents do. Arguing among siblings is normal."

The bottom line, when we left, was that we were relieved to hear that bickering was normal and figured we could cope somehow.

Afterward, though, I spoke with the counselor and told her I was having thoughts about whether Peter and I should consider getting back together. She felt he was amenable to considering it, too, and I decided to write Peter a letter broaching the possibility. In the nicest way, Peter let me know that he did not want to get back together. He wrote a note in reply, saying that too much water had passed under the bridge, and he did not believe we could rebuild our marriage. But he wrote, "Gail, fully aside from the kids, I care very much about your health, success and happiness. No matter what happens, in many ways I will be there for you." He added, "I also wanted to say what a happy, warm home you've made here. And thanks for Seattle—it's beautiful."

Peter was right. It would have been a mistake for us to get back together. Of course, I was hurt. I'd put myself out there and been rejected. (The counselor also felt badly, although she didn't need to.) But it was time for me to get on with my new life and to embrace the positive parenting relationship that Peter and I had created and that our three children deserved.

❦30

Divorce is, of course, an ending. And endings are often painful, even when they're for the best. Divorce inevitably brings change. As my sister, Alice, says, "Change is fun. You go first!" Divorce means the end of a broken marriage. It can bring about the end of other relationships as well—relationships with in-laws, friendships that depended on couples activities, membership in clubs and other social venues we used to frequent with our exes. But every ending is a beginning, and when we become divorced we get to choose new directions, new friendships. We need not feel like victims or walk around with our heads hanging in shame. We can take the reins in our own lives and create something new and better for ourselves. We can and should treat ourselves and others well, and demand (in a calm and positive way) that they treat us well, too.

As I've mentioned, before leaving Mill Valley I had a rapprochement with my father. Before that, I had made a commitment to myself that I would never let him run rough-shod over me again, and had set some basic ground rules that he'd have to follow in order to continue our relationship. He balked, and we ended up not seeing each other for five years. In truth, if I could have divorced my father, I would have and should have done so. But a toxic parental relationship is much more difficult to end than a bad marriage. Living in Seattle meant that I would inevitably need to deal with my father during holidays, baby showers, marriages, funerals, all the usual family occasions. By taking hold of the reins of my life, I would confront my father on my own terms and not let him dictate everything, as I had before cutting off contact with him. My father hated having me dictate rules to him. No one had dared cross him before. But even more, he detested being shut out of my life, so he reluctantly agreed to my rules of engagement.

Not long after we all moved to Seattle, I drove along Lake Sammamish, heading home after a visit with Linde. My Dad was in the car with me. He had been on his best behavior since helping me move. He had even paid for my move. Suddenly, out of the blue, my father said, "The craziest thing happened last night. I fell asleep on the couch while I was watching television, and when I awoke a few hours later, there was hard core porno on the television. This couple was really going at it." A wash of anger poured through me and I thought, "This is it. If I let him get away with this, I will have thrown out everything I've accomplished." I felt a hardening of resolve, and I will be forever proud of what I said and did next.

"STOP!" I said. "Do not say one more word to me about sex."

"HEY!" My father raised his voice and paused for emphasis. I felt the old flickers of fear flutter in my chest. "Don't act like I said something wrong! I just told you what I saw on television. And I won't be silenced by *you*!"

I let a pause hang between us and gripped the steering wheel. Then I said, "You just *were* silenced by me." I heard an edge of steel in my voice. "For forty years everyone in this family has tiptoed around you, trying to make sure we don't upset you. But from now on, you are going to tiptoe around trying to make sure you don't upset ME." My father sat in stunned silence. I did not look over at him, but I was on a roll. "Have you ever watched that television show called *Dynasty*?" I asked. Without giving him a chance to answer, I continued. "Well, there's a woman on that show named Alexis and she is a raving bitch. Everyone trembles when Alexis is mad. And from now on, that is how you are going to feel about ME. You are fired from the job of terrorizing everyone in this family."

My father and I rode the rest of the way to my house in silence. I was breathing hard and gripping the wheel and telling myself that Alexis would stick to her guns and I would, too. My dad got into his car and drove off as soon as we pulled into my driveway. I walked into my house, picked up the telephone and dialed his home number. I knew that he would not be there yet, and I could leave a message. This is what I said: "I know you aren't home and I am leaving you this message to follow up on what I just said in the car. Before I moved back to Seattle, I told you that you could never talk to me or my children about sex, my mother or religion. I meant it. If you ever mention those subjects to me again, I will walk out of your life and never look back. I will never even think of you again. You are through abusing me. We're having a family gathering here on Sunday. You may not come unless you agree to follow these rules. If you set one foot on my driveway, it means you agree to these rules. Goodbye." And I hung up. I was steamed up, but proud of myself. The little girl inside me was jumping up and down, screaming, "Yes! Yes! Yes!"

Sometimes in our lives we have to stand up for ourselves. The hardest thing I have ever done in my life was to stand up to my father. I had feared him for so long. I'd even believed that he might go so far as to murder me for daring to cut him out of my life or even draw emotional boundaries between us. But I had stood up to him.

My father came to the house the next Sunday and, for the most part, he followed my rules. Like a naughty child, he broke them here and there, espousing his atheistic views to my sons. I didn't care what my father believed, but I did not want him hammering away at my kids' minds. On more than one occasion, I had to sit him down at my table and lay it on the line. "Stop talking to everyone—especially my kids—about religion and sex! No one cares about your sex life or what you believe!" But he just wouldn't or couldn't behave. At a Mariners game or other public event, he often would blurt out some inappropriate comment and humiliate himself and, by extension, his family members. He found this immensely amusing. But I did not, and I finally did manage to shut him down. My father was afraid of me on some level, and he also had a new grudging respect for me. If he ever veered onto a subject I did not like, such as boring me for the thousandth time with his interpretation of *Finnegan's Wake*, I simply stood up and walked away, leaving him sitting there mid-sentence. I would no longer be his unwilling audience. My self-esteem shot up as a result of standing up for myself to the scariest person in my life. I told myself I was worth it. And I am.

❡31

From time to time, I've been asked how Peter and I dealt with each other after our divorce when we were angry or resentful with one another. "How did you handle it when you just wanted to kill him?" one young woman asked. I smiled before answering because she was so sincere, and because it had been a long time since I felt that kind of anger or resentment towards Peter. I'm glad I don't carry around that kind of baggage. A wise person once said, "Holding onto resentments is like drinking poison and hoping it kills the other guy." I don't know who coined the phrase, but he or she captured the essence of poisonous resentments. The resented person goes their merry way while the resentful one stews in toxic waste. I didn't want to be stuck in that kind of stew when I got divorced. But, for me, the *why* has always been more important than the *how* when it comes to getting along with Peter. At the core was a mutual decision to at least try to be helpful, not harmful, to our children and each other.

We had to grow up a bit and give up some petty habits. For example, when Peter and I were married, we said "No" to each other a lot. "Would you consider moving to Seattle? I'd like to be closer to my family," I'd ask.

"No. I don't think it would be good to live too close to your family. It will take up too much of your time," he'd answer. "I'd like to finish my PhD. I'd have to take a leave of absence to write my dissertation."

"No, that's not a good idea. You're already a partner in a law firm and we have kids. And we need a bigger house."

"I don't want a bigger house. This one is fine. What we need is more exercise. Would you like to play golf with me?"

"No. I don't like golf. Besides, it takes too much time. Why don't we go to Hawaii and get some sun?"

"No. I don't think we can afford it now."

Of course, we worked our way through many of these issues while we were still married. After a long time dragging my feet and resisting Peter's desire to finish his doctoral degree, I got it through my head that he'd never be satisfied if he didn't finish it, and I didn't want to be the one who'd stood in his way. We weren't always at cross-purposes when we were married, but we were at odds enough of the time and on so many issues—large and small—that our daily interactions often resembled negotiations. We kept mental score. We exhausted ourselves and each other. We drifted apart emotionally, withheld our affections and built up protective walls. So we had plenty of grist for the gripe-and-resentment mill. But somehow, after the shootings, everything changed. We didn't change who we were; I believe we were always two good people who had married and had had children in good faith. We didn't change our personalities. But we learned to say "Yes" more often after our divorce.

"I'd like to take the children to Texas to see my parents? Will that work for you?"

"Yes. That sounds like fun for the kids."

"Can we switch nights this week? Something has come up."

"Sure. No problem."

"I'm at the baseball game and I forgot to bring snacks. Can you stop by the store and get something?"

"Yes, I can."

After we divorced, our unspoken presumption was that the answer to any reasonable request would be "Yes."

The greatest concession Peter gave me after we divorced was to say yes when I begged him to move to Seattle so that I could be close to my family. I did my best to return his kindness. I allowed him to take the children to Texas for Christmas more than once. I walked the beach alone in Oregon one Christmas Day, watching families with children dancing along the waves. I felt lonely and depressed at the time, but I wanted Peter to share our children with his aging parents who had given so much of themselves and loved the children so deeply.

I have known divorced couples who rigidly clung to parenting schedules and seemed to take perverse pleasure in making each other's lives more difficult. Little Johnny had to be home in time for his nine o'clock bath or the world would come to an end. But who really wants to live their life that way? Instead of being obstacles in each other's lives, Peter and I gradually became the first backstop for one another. If I was running late to pick up the kids, I knew I could count on Peter to help me out—and vice versa. Did we continue to exasperate each other from time to time? Of course! Did we lose it occasionally? Yes.

Breakdowns happened—of course they did—but they became increasingly rare. And Peter and I made it a priority to get our equilibrium back after a bad day. Oddly enough, when we were married, it was harder to do so because we were trying to fix the underlying problems in the relationship. In a divorce, you just have to get along and treat each other courteously. It's a subtle but critical distinction.

※ ※ ※

Through my divorce from Peter, I learned something important about forgiveness. Previously I had thought forgiveness meant something like saying, "You did me wrong, but that's okay. I forgive you. I won't be mad anymore." But I learned that forgiving each other did not entail making a big list of all those wrongs and excusing them one by one. Forgiveness encompasses something much deeper. Over time, something loosened up inside me, and I became willing to give up being right. I knew that Peter was a good man, the father of my children, and my child-rearing partner. Sure, our marriage failed. Yes, we screwed up. No, we aren't perfect. Neither are our children. And neither is anyone else, whether single, married or divorced. I finally came to be at peace knowing my marriage with Peter was over forever. Our connection was now through our children.

❧32

After moving to Seattle, I wanted to expand my social circle, and Linde came into my office one morning with a flyer in her hand. She said that the downtown business and social club I had joined was organizing a ski trip to Switzerland. "I thought you might be interested in considering something like this," she said.

"Sign me up." I said.

"Um, do you want to take a look at the flyer or anything?"

"No," I said, looking up from my work. "I think I'll head downtown and buy a couple ski outfits." Retail therapy: my solution to everything.

I cured my fear of travel—at least to beautiful European destinations—on that trip to Switzerland. Our tour director had connections with the airline and invited me and one or two others from our group up to the flight deck of the 747 as we approached Copenhagen. After brief, pleasant exchanges with the pilots, we were allowed to look at the pilots' view as the plane skimmed low over the Baltic toward the runway. The sea and sky were midnight blue and tinged with pale pink light.

Sweden stretched to the north and Denmark to the south. The lights of Copenhagen sparkled in the distance, and my fears just fell away. I was with a group of new friends on this plane, headed for new adventures. Not everything had gone the way I'd planned, but the sun was faithfully rising over our beautiful planet.

I made some wonderful friends on that trip and also met a handsome Italian doctor. Zermatt is linked by chairlifts to Italy, and one day we skied from Switzerland to Cervinia, a stunning ski resort in northern Italy. As I zoomed past beautiful mountain hamlets under the Matterhorn, I wondered what had been wrong with me to fear travel. I skied a bit more slowly than the others, and this nice doctor stopped on the slope below, smiling and patiently watching me ski down. "You make me happy," he said when I caught up. I think he meant to say, "You make me laugh." The others in our group were more experienced skiers, and I pressed the limits of my abilities on that run into Italy. But the freedom was glorious.

After a delicious lunch in Cervinia, we had to catch the two o'clock chairlift in order to make all the connections to the top of the mountain where we could make our way back down into Switzerland. The doctor and I rode together on the long chairlifts and gondola rides. We spoke of literature, his travels to the United States, and of Firenze (Florence), his home. Later that night we danced. Fresh snow crunched under our feet as I walked back to the hotel with my new friends, laughing and saying goodbye. Stars twinkled over the Matterhorn, and the world seemed full of possibility.

My trip to Switzerland showed me something that we all know: it's easier to move on from a divorce when we meet someone new. The flip side, of course, is miserably true: it can be very painful to move on when only our ex finds someone new. Either way, though, we have to move on.

Sometimes on dark nights when I was alone, I could not find my way. I would wake from a deep sleep, unable to recall if my children were with me or not. I'd run down the hall to check. Unable to fall back to sleep (sometimes for hours), I'd feel sorry for myself for being alone and having to be separated so much of the time from my children. I knew I had to rebuild my life, and I'd look at the stars, wondering if they held promise for me. Twinkling in the distance, they seemed ancient and knowing. All the generations before us have contemplated them during arduous journeys. The constellations have long led sailors to safe harbor, marking a passage for those who have drifted from their course. I had drifted far from the course I'd envisioned for myself, and I wondered if I would ever get back. I wanted much more than a good divorce. I wanted love and connection with a man. I could not ask or expect my children to fill that void in my life.

In "Song of Songs," the man asks the woman to have faith:

> *If you can't find me, loveliest of all women,*
> *it's all right. Stay with your flocks.*
> *Lead your lambs to good pasture.*
> *Stay with your shepherd neighbors.*

I was alone, but I was doing my best to keep my children—my lambs—safe, and to surround them and myself with kind people. Our neighborhood was, indeed, filled with many wonderful "shepherd neighbors" who befriended our entire family and often praised Peter and my efforts to raise our children cooperatively. Only one person came right out and asked what the heck was going on—and he was a six-year-old boy! I was driving him home after a play date with Leigh.

"Why did you and Leigh's dad get divorced?" he asked from the back seat.

"Ah," I said, thinking quickly. "We decided we were meant to be friends."

"Well, if you can be friends, why couldn't you stay married?"

"We just decided we should be friends." This was my story and I was sticking to it. I looked in the rear view mirror and saw he wasn't buying it. I had to chuckle to myself. Out of the mouths of babes!

❡33

O ne of the challenges of co-parenting after divorce is that the financial status of the parents can diverge, making it difficult for one parent to match the lifestyle of the other. And although parenting is not a competition, it can feel like one after a divorce. In my case, I was especially eager to preserve my relationship with PJ and Ben, who loved their mom but who gravitated to the basketball court, drums, games and general boy-oriented fun at Peter's house.

❧❦

We hunger for the affections of our children not only because we deeply love them, but because we find validation of our worth from them. Children see the world from their own perspective, of course. A close friend of mine separated from her husband when their son was five and, even though she knew her son needed time with his father, she dreaded losing any time with her son, around whom her life revolved. She also feared that her son might love his father more because he was a boy and modeled himself after his father. Soon after her husband moved into an apartment, my friend's son came to her and said, "I want to live with Daddy."

"Why?" she asked, falling to her knees before him, crushed.

"Because he has an elevator!" he exclaimed.

As divorced parents, we need to keep in mind that our children love us regardless of whether we have an elevator. But in divorce, disparity between possessions, homes and incomes can present challenges. I had to suppress my urge to pull my children back and hold on too tight. After all, even if we can demand our "rightful" share of time, or command our children to stay with us at certain times, we can't capture our children's hearts and minds through a parenting plan or forced visits.

❧❧❧

By the time we moved to Seattle, Peter had dramatically shifted his professional focus and, even though he maintained his partnership with his law firm, he stopped practicing law. Instead, he pursued his business of developing and presenting large meetings around the country on health care, and he later developed an Internet-based business providing instruction and certifications on health care topics. He took significant financial risk in developing these businesses, and his efforts paid off handsomely. As a result, he was able to provide all kinds of material things and opportunities to the children that I was unable to match. Even though Peter was (and is still) generous with me and the children, I wanted to find and build a unique bond with each of my children.

❧❧❧

PJ was ten years old and beginning his transition from boyhood to adolescence the summer we moved to Seattle. One day he told me about a beautiful girl he'd met at the park. He was utterly smitten and could not get this lovely girl out of his mind. As PJ described the girl's beautiful hair and asked if I could help him find her telephone number, I told him his situation reminded me of *Romeo and Juliet*. PJ pressed me for details about this love story and said of Shakespeare, "I feel like I *know* him." I didn't know at the time that PJ would later pen award-winning poems, write and direct plays at Trinity College in Ireland, and write prolifically as an adult. But I recognized his early interest in literature and knew this was a plane on which we could relate to one another. PJ told me he wanted to read *Romeo and Juliet*, so I bought him a gold-leafed volume the next time I was in Barnes & Noble.

When I gave PJ his volume of *Romeo and Juliet*, he asked me to read it with him, and we sat down together on the couch. After we read for awhile, I needed to finish some chores and I slipped away to do something else, wondering whether PJ would be able to press on without me. Hours later, PJ showed up in the kitchen in a Superman costume asking if we could talk. We sat at the breakfast table and he looked at me with huge brown eyes. "Mercutio died!" he said. "Why do you think their families hated each other so much?" He looked so solemn and sincere. He was oblivious to the padded-chest Superman costume and red cape he was wearing.

I smiled and thought, "This is how it happens. Here is a boy placing a toe into a world of literature that will change him." As to Romeo and Juliet, I did my best to explain that in fighting over principles and power, their families had lost sight of what matters most in life. And they paid the ultimate price—the loss of their beloved children.

By the age of ten, PJ was a voracious reader and was often deeply moved by literature. When he was reading *Where the Red Fern Grows*, I tiptoed around the house dreading the moment when he reached the ending, where the boy's beloved coonhound dies. I'd see PJ coming and going from the kitchen for a drink or snack, and wonder if he'd finished the book and taken its ending in stride. I got my answer when I saw him walking toward me with stricken sadness on his face. He'd reached the end of the book and it had broken his heart, just like it had broken mine when I was young.

◈◈◈

It took me almost ten years to return to the story I had begun writing that fateful day I first took the boys to church. PJ was about fifteen when I finally finished the first two chapters. I told him I had been writing, and he asked to read what I'd written. I had shown it to no one and was nervous (but excited) to show my son my work.

"Well, it's only a draft," I said. "I mean, I plan to edit it a lot."

"That's okay," he said. "I'd really like to read it."

"Are you sure? It's pretty rough, of course."

"No, I mean it. I really want to read it."

"Well, okay." I handed my teenage son forty pages of my first real attempt at fiction. He smiled at me, turned around, walked into his bedroom and shut the door.

"You don't have to read the whole thing!" I called through his door. "It's probably pretty boring!"

"I'll talk to you later, Mom," he called back.

I paced around the house like an expectant father in a waiting room. That stuff I wrote is so dumb, I thought. The dialogue really sucks. I could hear every clock in the house ticking away the long seconds. Finally, finally PJ emerged from his bedroom. I stood in the kitchen with my back to him, trying to look nonchalant as I polished a hole through the countertop.

"Mom," he said. "I really like what you wrote."

I felt emotion tightening my throat. "Thank you, PJ. It's really not very good. But I appreciate your reading it."

"Don't say that about your writing, Mom. It really is good and I want you to finish it so I know what happens to your characters."

PJ has long since surpassed me in mastering classical works and in writing fiction. For his fifteenth birthday, I bought him a used set of the Harvard Classics, which he loved. He told me recently it's the best gift he ever received. In his lifetime he has written hundreds of poems, several screenplays, and is editing his first novel. I choose to believe he got his love of reading and writing from me.

◈

With Ben I have a bond of peace that began the morning after he was born, when we rested on the hospital bed and I told him how much he meant to me. That tiny boy already knew how to hug. With the exception of our brief war of wills over clothing, I cannot remember a cross word ever passing between us. Even when he did something wrong, I couldn't bring myself to really discipline him—except when he went through a very brief phase of showing he was too cool to wear his seat belt. This was on my Dr. Van Passion top-three list of rules that simply had to be enforced. Here is how I put that particular little phase to rest. The first time I noticed that Ben (who was about fourteen) was not wearing his seatbelt, I cheerfully but firmly reminded him to put it on. The second time, I said in a commanding officer tone, "Ben, put on your seatbelt." The third time, I slammed on the brakes, screeched to a sliding, fish-tailing stop, and said with a dead calm voice, "If I ever see you in a car without a seatbelt again, you won't drive a car until you are twenty-one. And if you don't believe me, TRY ME!" I screamed the last two words. That took care of that. Ben believed me—and well he should have.

But Ben was so good natured that I rarely got angry with him. When he veered off course, I'd try psychological tactics instead of outright confrontation. One late afternoon when the boys were in middle school, I got home from the grocery store and started unloading the groceries. When Ben walked through the kitchen, I asked him to please take out the garbage.

"No," he said.

"Why?" I asked, stopping what I was doing and looking at him. This didn't sound like Ben.

"I don't feel like it," he answered. He avoided my gaze, but cast off an impression of teenage rebelliousness. I did some quick thinking.

"Okay," I said, cheerfully. Ben sauntered out of the kitchen.

I put the food I had been planning to prepare in the refrigerator and got *People* magazine out of the grocery sack. I went to the couch, sat down, and started catching up on celebrity best-dressed lists and escapades. Not too much later, Ben walked up to me. "What's for dinner?" he asked.

"Nothing," I said pleasantly. I returned to my magazine.

"What? Why?"

"I don't feel like making anything," I said.

"Oh. Can I go to Paul's house then?"

"Sure."

"Okay. Can I have a ride?"

"No," I said, glancing up. "I don't feel like driving anywhere." I smiled and stretched casually. "I like this new way we're doing things around here. It really works for me." When Ben left the room, I sprinted to the phone and called Paul's mom. "Suzy," I said, "Paul's probably going to tell you Ben needs a ride and ask you to come get him." I filled her in briefly on what was going on. "Please don't give him a ride."

"No problem," she said, laughing. We stuck together on this. Soon enough, Ben had taken out the garbage and we were eating and driving again.

My approach to dealing with these types of daily issues was very different from Peter's. One of the things we and our children had to learn (and adjust to over time) was that the rules and parenting styles varied between the two households. Peter and I each did things in our own ways, and although we tried to maintain some loose consistency, we did not try to force each other into our own parenting mold.

When we first moved to Seattle, Leigh was three years old and my special bond with her was simply being a hands-on, loving mommy. By the time Leigh was five, she had come to realize that our family was different from her friends' families. It dawned on her that their moms and dads lived together and hers lived apart! She didn't like that one bit. She missed me when she was with Peter; and she missed him when she was with me.

"Mommy," she said one day when I picked her up at Peter's house, "I want you and Daddy to get married again." When I paused to think of an answer, she said, "I mean it!" My heart broke in two. My little girl threw her arms around my neck and said, "Mommy, pleeeeze. Marry Daddy again." Peter and I had been divorced for several years and, of course, we would never remarry. Leigh went through a short but intense depression when she finally understood that Peter and I would not be getting back together. I wanted to hold my little girl close—to make it up to her somehow. When Leigh was a bit older, I worked hard to indulge our mutual passion for Arabian horses; this was my way of forming one unforgettable bond with my daughter.

❧34

Peter's desire to take our kids traveling around the world was no idle fancy. He was serious, and he put his plans into action when the boys were eleven and nine. I was nervous and a wee bit jealous when he started planning a trip to Egypt.

"Don't worry," he said. "We're going on a tour with Abercrombie and Kent. They're the best tour operators in the world. We're going to cruise the Nile and go to the pyramids. I want the boys to see and appreciate ancient history."

My head was spinning. All of my fears about world travel rushed back into my head, and I worried I'd never see my sons again. But I knew I shouldn't stop my boys from going on such adventures with their dad. I had to deal with my own fears. Ultimately, I decided not to stand in Peter's way. To assuage my fears that they might be stranded in the desert with no water or not have basic first aid supplies if they got cut, I packed a suitcase full of supplies and insisted that Peter haul it along. I filled the suitcase with water bottles, foil-wrapped snacks, small bandages and the like. That would have to do.

While Peter and the boys were in Egypt, Leigh and I spent a couple of quiet weeks on our own. We missed the boys, and I felt a little sorry for us—we girls had been left behind. While rocking together on a patio chair, Leigh reminded me that our cat and our dog had both disappeared for a few weeks, but had eventually come home. "Romeo came back," she said. "Sofie came back. Maybe the boys will come back."

The boys did come back. And when they walked off that plane, Leigh and I were there to meet them. I dropped to my knees to hug them as if they had been gone for years instead of weeks. They were probably embarrassed, but I was so relieved. And what tales they had to tell of sailing the Nile, climbing the pyramids, PJ throwing up on the plane when it landed in Cairo!

"Guess what, Mom," Ben said with a huge smile. "Our taxi driver in Egypt fell asleep while we were driving 100 miles per hour!" I saw Peter and PJ exchange glances.

"Oh, he wasn't really asleep," Peter said. "He just nodded off for a second."

"Tell Mom about the cars with machine guns that followed us," Ben then suggested.

"Oh, those were security people hired by the tour operator," Peter said. "You know, just an abundance of caution."

Six weeks later, I read the horrifying news that gunmen had opened fire on foreign tourists at the temple on the Nile my sons had visited. The newspaper reported that anti-government extremists stabbed and slaughtered sixty innocent people at the Temple of Queen Hatshepsut: another gory bloodbath that members of my own family narrowly missed. What is wrong with this world? Who does these kinds of things? How can I let my children venture so far from home? This was and remains a huge struggle for me even now, when my children are grown.

It seems we had barely unpacked when Peter called me and broached the subject of travel again. "You know," he said, "when I got the air tickets for this last trip, they were having a promotion, and I got a free set of tickets to go around the world. The only catch is that we have to use the tickets within one year."

"Wait a minute," I said. "Are you telling me you want to take the boys on *another* big trip out of the country?"

"Well, I don't want to waste three tickets to go around the world."

"Where exactly do you plan on going this time?" I asked, with a knot of fear forming in my stomach.

"I was thinking about India."

Great, I thought. India. I had concerns that Peter's wanderlust was taking precedence over my children's safety. Why there? Why couldn't he just go to Paris or London? Everything had to be *huge*. And I had to suffer while they were gone. Peter wisely dropped the subject for a few months—but I knew he was moving forward with his plans.

Early that spring, Peter touched on the subject of those unused around-the-world plane tickets, and the word *India* crossed his lips more than once in my presence. In May, I opened the paper one morning and read that India had surprised the world by detonating five nuclear test bombs. That was it! I closed the paper and called Peter. "I will not allow you to take the boys to India," I said. "I will lie on the tarmac in front of the airplane, if necessary, to prevent you from doing it."

Peter also adhered to the principle of picking his battles, especially with me. "Fine," he said, "we may have to fly through Delhi, but we won't stay in India." Merely flying through Delhi was not my idea of a huge compromise, and I was still prepared to lie on the tarmac, if necessary, to stop the whole damn trip. Peter called me back after a couple of days. "Now, I know this might sound funny at first, but I am considering taking the boys to China and Vietnam. It's perfectly safe. I want them to see ancient cultures, and this is a great time to visit China. While we're over there, it will be cool to visit Vietnam, too." I grudgingly told him I'd think it over.

Again, I struggled with my competing emotions. I was angry with Peter for repeatedly pushing the envelope on adventuresome travels. But then I would think, "Would I have wanted to go on trips like that as a kid?" The answer was clearly yes. How would my sons feel later in life if they knew they could have seen more of the world and I was the one who stood in their way? One part of me wanted Peter to stop putting me in this difficult spot. But another knew my sons were lucky to have a dad willing and able to show them the world.

Peter called me one afternoon and made another proposal. (He was very good about giving me advance warning when working on a specific and concrete plan.) "I have an idea I'd like to run by you," he said. "I've put together a tentative tour to China for two weeks and then to Vietnam for two weeks this summer."

"A whole month?" I said, my voice rising.

"Yes," he said. "But please hear me out." I bit my tongue and held back feelings of jealousy, abandonment and fear. "I want these trips to be educational," Peter continued. "And this summer is a great time for the boys to learn. There's an amazing ancient civilization, the Minoans, that was discovered on the island of Crete—and I want the boys to see the ruins. I've found a cool rock castle on Crete that is available to rent. I think it would be nice to invite my parents and some friends, and I was thinking that you and Leigh could come over and stay for a month. There would be a lot of people, and I think you'd enjoy it."

I composed myself and sighed. But after thinking this proposal over for awhile, I agreed. I didn't want to be separated from the boys for two months, nor prevent them from going on the trip. "Okay," I told Peter. I purchased tickets for me and Leigh to fly to Crete.

❧❧❧

Ben called me three weeks into the trip. "I'm on China Beach, Mom!" he said. He sounded as if he missed me, and I wanted to cry. "The hotel is beautiful and the people are really nice," he said.

"Are you having fun and learning a lot?" I asked.

"Yes," Ben said. "PJ and I crawled in the Cu Chi Tunnels and we went to a museum from the Vietnam War." Well, I thought, at least their minds are being stretched. But I have claustrophobia, and the thought of PJ and Ben in underground tunnels on a battlefield halfway around the world made me shiver.

About a week later, Leigh and I boarded a jet and embarked upon a convoluted airline trip to Crete (only *I* could have arranged such a ridiculous and long route that involved several plane changes and even required us to change airports in Athens). Leigh, who turned five on that trip, was an amazingly good little traveler, keeping a smile on her face the whole way until we climbed into a hot taxi in Athens and then boarded a tiny propeller plane bound for Crete. Exhaustion overcame her as we landed in Crete, and she burst out crying, refusing to get off the plane. When I finally coaxed Leigh down the steps and we straggled into the tiny terminal, she was thrilled to see her brothers and her dad waiting for her, laden with gifts. She jumped into their arms, accepting their eager hugs and kisses and forgetting her exhaustion.

"Hi Mom," the boys smiled and hugged me.

"Hi Gail," Peter said. We exchanged back-pats. "Welcome to Crete. Let's get your bags."

¶35

Peter had rented the Villa Aghios Nikolaos, also known as the Crete Rock Castle. Peter told me as we rode in the van that the castle had been built on the ruins of a 16th century Venetian fortress and was now owned by a Greek movie director. He said the movie director's former wife and little girl were staying in a private apartment in a separate building on the property. Rumor had it, he said, that James Cameron and family had just vacated the castle. Cameron had recently completed directing the movie *Titanic*. Peter had invited more than thirty guests, including his parents, friends from law school, Roy and Amy and their kids, my sister and sister-in-law, two nieces, friends from Seattle—lots and lots of people. As we drove for an hour across the island to Aghios Nikolaos, he told me who was coming when. When we pulled up to a castle perched on a cliff overlooking the Mediterranean, I was impressed. When I saw the terrace, I felt worse. The large stone terrace was edged with a low rim rising barely past my ankles. Hundreds of feet below the terrace, the sea washed against the vertical stone walls. I practically crushed Leigh against my chest. Peter saw my alarm and told me not to worry. He had gotten a nanny to help supervise Leigh. I was not comforted.

That Crete trip was strange for me. The kids ran around the castle having the time of their lives. I was with my extended family, but I felt diminished. I was one guest among many on my own children's vacation. I sat under the olive trees on a chaise overlooking the sea, watching Leigh. The first morning, as Leigh played next to me, a tiny sprite of a child with dark hair and eyes appeared next to us.

"Hello," I said, smiling. Leigh stood up and the girls looked at each other. Soon a lovely Greek woman rounded the corner and walked up to us. She introduced herself as Soteria, and I realized that she must be the Greek movie director's former wife. We exchanged brief small talk, and the girls sat down and started playing. Soteria spoke perfect English, of course. This was fortunate because, to my embarrassment, I was unable to utter a syllable of Greek; I hadn't even managed to master "please" or "thank you."

Leigh and Soteria's daughter made fast friends, although neither spoke the other's language. They scampered together and giggled in the universal language of small children. One horrifying morning, though, soon after we arrived, the girls began running toward the edge of the terrace, curls flying behind them. I yelled at Leigh to STOP as they raced toward the ledge. Leigh paused momentarily, knowing I meant business, but then flung a mischievous glance over her shoulder and continued running toward the rock rim. I had levitated from my chaise lounge when I first yelled, and I now bounded across the stone terrace, chasing my daughter. I caught her mere feet from the precipitous plunge. Waves smashed against the rocks below us and, in my mind's eye, I saw my baby girl falling into the sea. Whack! I smacked Leigh's bare thigh with a furious slap—the only time I recall striking her. I don't favor corporal punishment, but I will confess that I've used it as a last resort a few times. This was one of them. And right or wrong, I don't regret having spanked Leigh that morning, because she never approached that ledge again. But in years to come, Leigh would occasionally delight in asking me in front of others, "Remember when you beat me?"

Each night at Aghios Nikolaos, Peter and his guests shared dinner at a long table in the dining room. Peter's parents and several of their friends were there. As much as Peter's parents and I still loved each other, we all felt awkward because of the divorce. The tension was heightened when I was joined by a pilot with whom I had started a relationship. I'll call him Clint. He and Peter had met and got along fine. Peter extended an invitation to Clint to join us on Crete. Peter was dating a lot, and we had both moved on. But Peter's mom had not. Things had not yet smoothed back into the warm and loving relationship we would eventually re-establish. Seeing me ride off on the back of a motorcycle with Clint took Peter's mom awhile to get used to. Peter's sailing off with a Greek-American woman for a week's affair didn't sit well either. Peter's mom was forced to adjust to some difficult changes, but she went along with our efforts to get along for the sake of the children. We all focused on other things. The dinner table was full of friends and family, and conversation centered on everyone's travels.

"You won't believe what happened while we were in Vietnam," PJ said one evening. "We had a great tour guide in Ho Chi Minh City. He took us everywhere and we really liked each other. He invited us to his home. His whole family could ride on one motor scooter and they lived in just two rooms. When we got to their house, I just about fell over because I saw a picture of Cotty on the wall."

"Cotty? Are you talking about your friend from fifth grade in Mill Valley?" I asked.

"Yes," PJ said, laughing. "Cotty!" To PJ's amazement, his Vietnamese tour guide had previously guided the family of his elementary schoolmate on a tour of Vietnam, and had enjoyed the experience enough to place Cotty's picture on his wall. What an amazingly small world, I thought. And if I'm crazy to let my kids venture so deeply into this world, at least one other Mill Valley mom is, too.

Many friends and family members came to the Rock Castle on Crete, but I continued to feel out of step. I was with my children, but they were not on my watch. Before Clint arrived, I spent a lot of time relaxing under the olive tree. Soteria sometimes joined me; we talked, and I found her to be a fascinating woman. We seemed to have similar views on many things. Each morning, she swam in the cove beneath the cliffs, wearing a snorkel and taking long, easy strokes. I joined her once or twice, feeling akin to her. Here we were, I thought, two women bobbing at sea beneath a towering castle where our wealthy ex-husbands were able to entertain our children.

Amy and Roy came to visit, and I enjoyed their company immensely. But when they left, I was forlorn and wanted to leave, too. That night, I became ill. I vomited after dinner and thought I had gotten food poisoning. All night long, I struggled with increasing illness and could find no relief. By the time the sun was rising, I knew I needed medical help, and Clint helped me crawl up the steps to the top of the castle, where Peter was staying. Within a short time, I was checking into the hospital at Aghios Nikolaos. Fortunately, many of the doctors and staff members spoke English, and they tried to diagnose what was wrong with me. All day long, they observed me and performed various tests, but I was not improving and they had no answers. Clint stayed with me at the hospital, and visitors from the Rock Castle kept stopping by to monitor my progress. Finally, about eight o'clock that night, a doctor I hadn't seen before strode into my room accompanied by an entourage of doctors and nurses, all of whom had been tending to me throughout the day.

"Hello," he said. "How do you feel?"

"Not well," I answered.

He pressed his fingers to my abdomen and quickly released them, as others had done all day. This time a sharp pain ricocheted through me and I yowled.

"Did it hurt when I pressed or released?" he asked.

"When you released!" I answered.

"You have appendicitis," he said. "You need surgery."

"What? When?" I asked, flabbergasted.

"Soon. We will get you ready right now."

I felt panicky. "Well, I need to say three things before you operate on me," I said.

"What are they?"

"First," I said, "I am a mom. I have three children. I must wake up from this."

"Do not worry," he said. "What is next?"

"I don't want to feel this surgery. I saw something on television about people being awake during surgery. Please make sure I'm asleep."

"Do not worry," he said. "What is next?"

"Well, I hope I don't have a big scar. You know . . . "

The doctor waved his hand dismissively. "This is the least of your worries," he said. With that, he turned on his heel and marched out of the room with his entourage behind him. All except one stern-faced nurse.

Clint pressed my hand. "I'm sorry," he said. "I love you and I don't want anything bad to happen to you." He rushed off to call Peter and let him know what was going on.

Peter popped into the room just before I was wheeled away. "How are you?"

"I'm having surgery!" I said.

"I'm sorry, Gail. I love you and I don't want anything bad to happen to you." The stern-faced nurse looked slightly confused. Peter continued looking at me with concern and sympathy. Within moments, I was on a gurney rolling into an operating room with big Greek letters over the doorway. The only Greek I knew was Kappa Kappa Gamma and Gamma Phi Beta. My sorority days had not prepared me for this.

The anesthesiologist peered at me with kind eyes over a green paper mask in the operating room. "I get really sick from anesthesia," I told him.

"Oh," he said, rolling his eyes. "Not here!" He placed a mask over my face and I disappeared into a black hole. I swear, I woke up just moments later and it was over. I was still in the operating room and I saw several masked faces staring down at me. "How do you feel?" the anesthesiologist asked. I recognized his kind eyes.

"I feel okay." I smiled weakly back at him. "Thank you." And I did feel okay. I never felt sick. With the help of these strangers, I had handled my appendectomy in a foreign country with flying colors. When I was wheeled back into my room, the walls were covered with pictures drawn by my children telling me they loved me and wanted me to feel better and come back soon.

Peter and Clint came to see me soon after I was taken back to my room. "Soteria was so worried about you," Peter said. "She leapt into action and arranged to have a special surgeon brought in to do your surgery."

Only much later did I learn from one of my friends, a Greek-American who arrived at the castle after I left, that Soteria had arranged for one of the best surgeons in Greece to come to Aghios Nikolaus to take care of me. Unfortunately, by the time I was released from the hospital, Soteria had already returned with her daughter to Athens, and I never got to thank her for her kindness. Do you know what the name Soteria means? It translates to "goddess of safety and protection from harm." Thank you, Soteria. You saved my life!

My health insurance covered me anywhere in the world, but Peter learned that we would be required to pay for my surgery and hospital stay in cash before I was released from the hospital. He and his house guests scrambled to pool together their travelers checks, credit cards, whatever might be required to bail me out of the hospital. We didn't know the size of the bill, but were certain it would reach into the thousands for emergency surgery, a three-day hospital stay, and all the drugs and care required. I waited in my room while Peter and Clint headed to face the music with the cashier. All told, the charges, including the services of a famous surgeon, came to less than $300! Peter was able to make the payment.

❧❧

As time passed, I hoped that Peter had given up on the idea of taking the boys to India, but the answer was *no*. Peter was relentless. The India trip tested our cooperative compact to the max, but it was a great experience for our sons. The year after the trip to China, Vietnam and Crete, Peter told me he wanted to take the boys to India. They hadn't blown anyone up with nukes, they were at peace, and Abercrombie and Kent would make sure everything was fine. Reluctantly, I relented. Leigh and I spent Christmas alone and missed PJ's birthday, too. Once again, after they were safely back, I was glad they had gone.

After returning from India, Ben told me a story that taught me that these trips were not just adventures, but life-changing experiences. While heading to the Delhi airport, Ben said, he was looking out the car window, and was struck by the sight of beggars in rags along the road. He had never seen such poverty at home, and he became aware of the rupees touching his hand in his pocket. As their car stopped at a crowded intersection,

Ben's eyes fell on a woman sitting cross-legged on the sidewalk and holding a baby wrapped in rags. He said in a split second, he decided he wanted her to have his rupees, and he jumped out of the car and ran to the woman. "I put the rupees in her hand," he said, "and when she looked at me, I knew we would never forget each other."

❡36

Peter and I have different parenting styles, although our core values are similar. Neither one of us is a strict disciplinarian, although Peter is more willing than I to ride herd on the kids to do chores and get things done. I found it was easier to do a lot of those things myself. I know this was a cop-out, but it has always been hard for me to make my kids do things they don't want to do. In my opinion, we baby boomers have some deep-seated fear that our kids won't love us if we lay down the law. In truth, the worst parent-child relationships I have witnessed are those in which overbearing parents make their children's lives miserable with countless rules, frequent punishments and constant nagging. There are no easy answers and, within reason, each parent must find his or her own way.

Peter and I both worked at discipline, and even consulted a counselor about this issue. From time to time, he would yell at the kids to clean their rooms, but they knew he was a paper tiger. Peter told me more than once that he and Ben would lock horns over chores—and Ben could be very stubborn. Peter turned to me for advice on how to deal with Ben's gentle but intractable stance over one thing or another. I couldn't offer much help—Ben was a perfect peach for me. Peter and I couldn't help laughing as he told me once that he'd locked himself in his own bedroom after Ben flatly refused to accommodate some simple, reasonable request. To add insult to injury, Ben got his trumpet out and blew a long, defiant wail outside of Peter's bedroom door.

❧❧

Like many kids of my generation, I had known better than to engage in direct battles with my parents. I have always known my parents love me, but neither liked criticism—you just didn't go there. On the other hand, neither parent criticized me and no one micro-managed my life. On the contrary, I had great freedom and, after the initial upheaval of my parents' divorce, my day-to-day existence became pretty calm and secure. My mom was a wonderful homemaker and an excellent cook. She's eighty-seven years old now and still has a beautiful home, wears elegant clothing and cooks delicious meals. She takes good care of herself and sets a great example for her eight adult children and step-children, ten grandchildren, and five great-grandchildren.

My mom was always supportive of my good grades at school, but I doubt she ever set foot in a PTA meeting. Once each year, she went to the teacher-parent conference expecting to hear good news, and I made sure she did. She wouldn't have brooked anything else, and she checked my report cards to make sure I maintained high grades. Because I did, she gave me incredibly loose rein, even allowing me to skip school whenever I wanted, which was every other Monday. I liked the positive response I got for good work. My mom graduated magna cum laude from the University of Washington; her poetry was published in the UW paper. But when she was done with her schooling, she was done with school, period. She cheerfully gave help when asked, but generally left me and my siblings to manage our own day-to-day homework and outside activities.

My dad, to his credit, taught me I was capable and smart. He barely would have known where my school was located and certainly never attended any school functions. (To be fair, he once came to Father's Weekend at my sorority in college, and he even behaved. Thank God.) He read out loud to me—starting when I was twelve, with *All Quiet on the Western Front* by Erich Maria Remarque. I loved literature and my father later told me, "I knew you were smart when we read that first book together." He spoke endlessly (exasperatingly, repetitively) of Shakespeare, Camus, and James Joyce until I thought I would commit suicide if I ever heard the words *Finnegan's Wake* again.

But my father valued education. He told me from day one that I was smart and that he would pay for my college education. When I announced to him early in my senior year of high school that I had applied and been accepted to the University of Colorado, he laughed, got out his checkbook and asked me, "How much do you need?" It wasn't as if he was wealthy. Far from it. But he gave what he could toward my education and, even if he later took a bit more credit than he should have ("I put *all four* of my kids through college!"), he certainly never complained about his contributions, which were generous.

Peter, on the other hand, was an only child of a doting mother who was intimately involved in every detail of his young life. He'd had a strict upbringing based on routines and clearly set-out rules. His parents were stable, churchgoing (she was) and very focused on their main mission, which was to provide their only son with opportunities, education, stability and love. Their unwavering emotional and financial support helped Peter achieve great academic success, including his law degree and Harvard PhD. Peter's eighty-nine-year-old mother lives in the same Texas house Peter grew up in, and PJ, Ben and Leigh still love to visit her. Peter's parenting style is loosely modeled on his parents' style. He, too, is heavily involved in the kids' day-to-day schooling, and he notes their every event on his already packed calendar. He has high educational expectations and is willing to fund almost any academic endeavor. While I would be the one to volunteer in the classroom and make snacks for team sports, Peter would regularly remind me of upcoming events, opportunities and deadlines. He's been the one to arrange tutors, summer programs, pre-planned vacations and the like. I believe a lot of that came from being an only child whose life was closely managed when he was young.

Our different backgrounds and parenting styles partially explain why our marriage was difficult, but interestingly, these differences helped our divorce work well. I couldn't handle getting out of bed at seven o'clock on a Sunday morning to greet Peter, armed with a calendar in his hand, wanting to schedule stuff for the kids. I just wanted a strong cup of black coffee and the newspaper. When we had separate houses, I could live according to my own rhythm and so could Peter. The kids easily segued back and forth. As Leigh once put it, "I love the difference between my parents' styles. With Dad, we have tons of activities that I love, and with Mom, I can just chill."

I can't help but laugh when I look back at photo albums. As much as Peter loves order, he could never tackle Leigh's waist-length curls. Her nursery school teacher once told me they would chuckle when she arrived at school and say to each other, "It's a 'Mom Day' or a 'Dad Day'", depending upon whether her hair was in neat braids or a wild halo. Peter attempted to solve this dilemma by taking her to Supercuts for a wash and braid on Saturdays. They were "regulars," and she got some gorgeous braids done there. Hey, different strokes for different folks. Peter and I gave each other some slack, and we tried to keep a sense of humor about it when we could.

As hard as we worked to cooperate, co-parenting was not stress-free. From the day she was born, Leigh and I have been very close. We are similar in many respects, except I am an introvert and she is an extrovert. No one—and I do mean *no one*—enjoys throwing large parties more than my daughter. Over the years, Peter hosted many large parties for Leigh. Both knew that I didn't approve of all those parties. But that helped to form *their* special bond. And, lo and behold, it appears I was wrong to discourage Leigh's interest in parties. She is now an intern at a publicity firm in Hollywood, helping with celebrity events, thrilled to be able to escort stars on the red carpet. "I had to work so hard to be allowed to work an event," she proudly told me. "But now they're asking me to do lots of them!"

❧37

When our kids were growing up, we were fortunate to have an excellent public high school near us. The high school was one of the primary reasons we chose the neighborhood when we moved to Seattle. But getting kids successfully through high school can be a significant challenge. We encountered some of these challenges, and Peter and I had to work together to deal with them.

PJ was, of course, our first to enter high school. The teachers were excellent overall. But we had a few bad experiences. We had encouraged PJ to sign up for debate in ninth grade because of his love for engaging conversation. He did so, and joined a class that had a range of students from ninth through twelfth grades. The teacher had no previous experience teaching debate. The first assignment was to select a topic of the students' choice, pick a side of an argument, and stand before the class to give the argument. Because each student picked his own the topic, there was no opponent on this first debating assignment.

PJ decided that the long-running problems in Northern Ireland would be an interesting topic. He prepared his argument and was among the first to stand before the class to make his speech. He argued, in short, that the English had no business in Ireland. As he finished his speech and sat down, the teacher lit into him. In front of the entire class, she said that if he had been at a debating competition, he would have failed. Why? This teacher said that her grandparents were English, and that the English had every right to be in Ireland. She accordingly would be giving PJ a D for his argument.

I was outraged and wanted to talk to the teacher. But PJ said he preferred to handle it himself. The teacher told him she would eliminate his *D* by allowing him to observe a debate at another school. He was to come to school at seven o'clock Saturday morning, dressed in a suit, ready to get on the bus and go. PJ and I were up and eating breakfast by six o'clock that Saturday morning, and he got into his suit, looking miserable but resolute. I, quite frankly, was madder than a wet hen, but was biting my tongue. We drove to the high school and arrived by 6:45, but could see no sign of a bus or of any activity whatsoever. We drove around and around the school, looking in all of the parking lots for a bus or the other debaters. PJ got out of the car and walked in his suit to the school doors, which were locked tight. Finally, after the departure time had long since come and gone, we went home. We both worried for the rest of the weekend that PJ had mixed up his instructions and had missed the bus and his opportunity to expunge his poor grade.

On Monday afternoon, when PJ came home from school, I asked him if he'd discovered what had happened.

"The teacher said the debate was cancelled," he said.

"You must be kidding," I said. "Did she apologize to you?"

"No," he said. "She just said it was cancelled."

"She is an idiot," I said.

PJ also had excellent teachers at the school, but the debating experience—along with a few other instances in which it appeared that independent thought was discouraged—dampened his intellectual enthusiasm, at least in respect to school, leaving him more inclined to play the class clown. But Peter and I both made no bones about the fact that he had to behave, like it or not.

By the tenth grade, PJ had given up interest in impressing the teachers and entertained himself by amusing the other students. The students thought he was hilarious, and even the teachers admitted he was quite funny. But it became a problem on more than one occasion when he interrupted instruction with his pranks. His PE teacher called me one time to report that PJ was clowning around too much. I spoke to him about it and said he needed to knock it off. But soon afterward, I got another call from the teacher (who called PJ "Peter"). Our conversation went something like this:

"I'm having trouble with Peter again. All the kids have to complete a two-mile run on the track. Peter completed his run easily the first day, but some of the other kids have to work up to it. The ones who are finished are supposed to be doing something else, but Peter keeps running backwards on the track, making the kids laugh and interrupting their runs. I can't make him stop and wonder if you can give me some help."

"No problem," I said. "You will never have this problem with Peter again. I can guarantee it. In the remote chance that you ever have to call me again, I will come up and stand by the track and make sure he does not interfere with the class."

"Wow," the teacher said. "Thanks."

Here is a little secret on how to terrify a teenager in a way that cannot get you into legal trouble. I pulled this one out of the bag because I didn't want to hear from that PE teacher again. My follow-up conversation with PJ went something like this:

"Hi, PJ, how was school today?"

"Fine."

"Good. Anything special happen?" I asked this question every day and always got the same answer.

"Nope."

"Really. That's interesting. Because your PE teacher called me today."

Pause. "Oh."

"PJ, have you ever seen hair rollers?"

"Um, I don't think so. What are they?"

"Hair rollers are little pink spongy things that women use to curl their hair. We don't wear hair rollers in public because they look really stupid."

PJ's eyes widened as I let him wonder where the hell this conversation was headed.

"Anyway," I continued in a pleasant voice, "Your PE teacher has called me twice now and complained that you are interrupting class by running backwards down the track and making other kids laugh. I think it's great to be funny, but I am not going to allow you to interrupt the teacher and other kids. So if your PE teacher ever calls me to complain about you again, I am going to roll my hair up in pink hair rollers and come to school in my bathrobe and stand by the side of the track and make sure you don't bother anyone."

PJ looked at me with a wary, amused look that had just that right mixture of fear in it. I could see the wheels turning in his mind. Would she really do that? The funny thing was that he believed I was pulling his leg, but just the slimmest reed of potential for such a humiliation stopped him dead in his tracks (no pun intended). I never heard from the PE teacher again.

For a brief stint, we decided PJ should have a job. Peter and I had both held down jobs in high school and had been responsible for earning our own spending money. Peter bagged groceries for years at the local grocery store. I babysat, cleaned houses and worked at a dental office. We wanted our kids to know the value of work. And PJ was agreeable! Soon enough he landed a job at a local movie theater—a chain that operated up and down the West Coast. I dropped him off in front of the theater his first evening on the job, telling him I'd pick him up there at the end of his shift. He walked into the theater wearing his white shirt and maroon polyester vest.

"How was it?" I asked at midnight when he got in the car, along with the powerful aroma of buttered popcorn.

"Fine," he said. "I had to learn to add fast and to give change. But most of the time during the movies we just stood around talking."

"Really? Who did you talk to? What did you talk about?"

"Oh, I talked to my boss. I asked him if he'd ever thought about starting a union. I told him if they banded together they could probably get better pay."

"What? Oh my gosh! What did he say?"

"He said no. He'd never thought about it."

"Wow," I said. "You might want to save the topic of unionizing for a little later."

¶38

PJ worked diligently at the theater, as we'd asked him to do, but Peter and I both worried that he wasn't thriving in school. We talked about ways to inspire him, and Peter came up with the idea of hiring an educational consultant to help us explore possibilities. Peter, PJ and I went to the first meeting with the consultant one rainy afternoon, and PJ sprawled casually back in a chair, looking only mildly interested in the conversation. But when the consultant asked whether he had ever thought about studying overseas, PJ sat forward and perked up.

"That sounds interesting," he said. PJ had loved his travels with his dad.

The counselor told us England and Scotland had great schools for English-speaking students from abroad. He put Peter in touch with an educational consultant in London and, from our respective homes, Peter and I had several conference calls with him about various schools. PJ was eager to explore the possibilities, and Peter hired the consultant to arrange interviews. The three of us made plans to visit independent schools from the southern tip of England to the northern coast of Scotland. Peter hired a driver and made all of the hotel arrangements. I flew separately to meet them in London.

Peter had purchased accommodations for me in each of the hotels for the week. He and PJ stayed together. When I arrived at the hotel in London, Peter told me with typical enthusiasm, "I got you and PJ tickets to *The Lion King* for tonight." I thought I would pass out from jet lag, but within the hour, we three were having afternoon tea and cucumber sandwiches in the hotel. Then PJ and I set off for the performance, jet lag be damned.

Peter and I agreed that it was wonderful to have time together, just the two of us with PJ. The next morning, we were picked up by a charming English driver who expertly—and swiftly—ushered us along the back roads from one school to the next. The schools were diverse. I particularly liked Millfield in Somerset. It had great facilities and single rooms. Millfield required chapel attendance only once a week, whereas the other schools required chapel attendance every morning. I wanted PJ to have a better exposure to religion than we had provided, but I did not want him starting each day resisting chapel attendance.

PJ liked all of the schools we visited in England, as did Peter and I. The last two schools we visited were in Scotland. When we pulled into Fettes College in Edinburgh, I had a mixed reaction. Rumor had it the school's Gothic architecture was the inspiration for Hogwarts in *Harry Potter*. I thought, "This place scares me because it is huge, spooky-looking and too far from home." My next thought was, "He's going to pick this school. I just know it." And pick it he did.

"How will you feel about attending chapel each morning?" I asked.

"It will be a nice time to reflect," he said. "I can choose to believe what I want."

PJ spent the next two years at Fettes, where he hit his groove and made friends from all over the world. Although he'd been cut from the basketball team at home for failing to show up at summer practices, he coached the Fettes team (comprised mostly of young men from China) to a championship in Scotland. He became the debating champion of the school. He started a poet's society. He made a chapel speech on love, which his housemaster said was the best student speech he'd heard in thirteen years. He made another chapel speech that offended some teachers who found it irreverent, causing them to stand up and walk out of the chapel. (PJ later let me read that speech, and I loved it. I thought it was warm, funny and inclusive, and would appeal to God's sense of humor.)

PJ cast and directed the play *Robin Hood* during his second year at Fettes. Peter, Ben and I traveled to Scotland to watch the Friday night opening of the play. Fortunately, we missed the Saturday night performance, when the sword-play went awry and the tip of a sword broke off, spun through the air, and hit the headmaster's ten-year-old son in the forehead. A ghastly silence fell over the theater, but when the headmaster's son stood up and cheered for Robin Hood, everyone else did, too, and the play carried on.

I was grateful to Peter for making these opportunities available to our children. Watching PJ graduate from Fettes to the accompaniment of Scottish bagpipes and drums was a thrilling experience, not just because he had succeeded with flying colors, but because Peter and I had triumphed, too. We had lifted our son from his doldrums in school. We were friends, working in the best interests of our children. We were long since divorced—but there we were, celebrating a huge milestone together with our kids.

During our last trip to Edinburgh, we were invited to a party given by the parents of one of PJ's school friends. The family boasted a long line of Fettesians and put on a beautiful party at their Edinburgh flat. Soon after arriving at the party, we met the parents of another friend—the mother a strikingly pretty Italian who towered over her Scottish husband. When Peter and I casually told them we were divorced, they laughed and then lowered their voices. "I wouldn't mention that *here*," the man said with a wink and nod toward the host.

"Oh, okay," we said. It was no big deal to us one way or the other, but it was clear our status as a friendly divorced couple could be considered weird or worse in present company. We had a great time at the party and later at dinner with the Italian/Scottish family. A couple years later, PJ visited his friend in Italy. When he returned, he casually mentioned over his welcome-home dinner that his friend's parents had gotten divorced.

"Oh my gosh," I said, surprised. "Are they doing okay? Are they getting along?"

"I think so," PJ said. He looked up from his plate. "By the way, it's great to be home eating your spaghetti again, Mom. You could sell this sauce in Italy!"

❧39

Ben loved high school from the day he started. He wore the school colors, started a band, participated in leadership, and held an office. The biggest challenge Peter and I faced with Ben in high school was that he was too well liked by older kids, and we worried that he might be exposed to too much, too soon. We were amused but slightly concerned when Ben was invited by the varsity girls' swimming team to be their manager when he was a freshman. He wasn't even a particularly great swimmer. I couldn't figure out what was going on.

"What did you say?" I asked him somewhat incredulously when he told me he had received the invitation.

"Are you kidding?" he answered. "I said yes!" He later told me that the girls' bus driver had looked at him funny when he got on the bus before the team's first swim meet and said, "What are you doing here?"

"I'm the team manager," Ben said. He traveled with the girls to all their meets. Senior girls came to visit him at our house. Of course, as his mom I adored him, but I couldn't quite figure out his pied-piper quality. He was cute, sweet and sincere, with no trace of arrogance or swagger. People simply gravitated toward him.

When Ben was in ninth grade, he joined the junior varsity basketball team and was off to a good start making three-point shots. But early in the season he took a charge during a game and broke his wrist badly. He was knocked out of playing for the season, but his wrist healed and he came back to the team the next year. I found it frustrating, because Ben spent a lot of time on the bench that year and the next, and I resented the way playing time was allocated by the coaches. But Ben was a great sport, and he progressed to the varsity team. Still, he sat on the bench, and I had to keep my opinions to myself. I perched on the bleachers many times with a fake look of enthusiasm on my face while Ben waited for an opportunity to play. He was unfailingly enthusiastic, though. Each and every time the team ran from the floor to the bench for a huddle, Ben would leap up and high-five everyone with a big smile on his face.

"Basketball isn't the only sport, you know," I once said. "If you quit the team you'd be able to go snowboarding on the weekends."

"No," Ben said. "I love basketball and I don't want to quit."

Sometimes I was tempted after a game to call the coach and let him know how I thought he should run things. But given that I couldn't even keep score correctly, my advice wouldn't have meant much. More importantly, Ben would have freaked out if I'd butted into his business like that. "How does he do it?" I asked Peter during one particularly aggravating game.

"He's a good boy," Peter said.

At the end of Ben's senior year, I went to his school for the basketball awards ceremony and was relieved when Ben's final season was over. Many awards were handed out that afternoon as coaches and players were recognized for their contributions: the most points, the most free-throws, et cetera. Finally, all of the parents were called out onto the gym floor and handed roses by their sons. Peter and I stood next to each other with roses in our hands. Then came the announcement: "The next award goes to the member of the team voted by the coaches and the team to be the most inspirational player." The head coach called out Ben's name. I was humbled and proud and felt a lump in my throat. "And finally," the coach said, "we are proud to announce the sportsmanship award for the varsity team." Again, he called out my son's name. As Ben accepted these awards, his teammates jumped up and high-fived and whooped, just as Ben had done so many times for them. I learned a tremendous lesson about sportsmanship and humility from my son through that experience.

❧❧

When Ben was a junior in high school, Peter offered him the opportunity to study abroad. The three of us made a whirlwind tour of several schools in England and Scotland—with the same charming driver—and Ben was offered admission by several schools. I knew Peter would have loved for Ben to go, but Ben was happy with his high school and close friendships and didn't want to change schools. I was glad, and Peter graciously respected Ben's choice. By then, PJ was thinking of staying overseas for college. He ultimately spent four years at Trinity

College in Dublin and was away from home for six years in all. He came home on frequent vacations, and I knew he had found a niche that suited him well. But one son in Europe was plenty for me.

Peter gave Ben the opportunity to do a summer program at Yale after his first year of college. Unlike PJ, Ben was not used to being far from home. He called me on the Fourth of July from the dorm at Yale, sounding down.

"No one else is even here yet," he said. "What if I don't meet anyone? What if I don't make any friends?"

"It's Yale," I said, "not a prison. If you want to come home, I'll buy you a ticket."

"No," he said, "I don't want to quit." A couple days later, I again asked how it was going. "I like it a lot," he said. "I've been going out into the neighborhoods around the school, and I've found some really good basketball pick-up games. I like the guys and it's a lot of fun."

"Wow," I thought. That's Ben. Then a couple days later, we spoke again. His voice was happy and confident.

"Yeah, Mom," he said, sounding cool. "I'll talk to you soon, okay? I'm with some friends in New York City. We're staying at this girl's dad's apartment in Manhattan." So much for not making friends.

❧40

When divorced parents share custody of their children, as Peter and I have, both parents necessarily spend a significant amount of time separated from their children. I often struggled with the feeling that I was losing precious time with my kids, but I tried to cope in positive ways, with the goal of forging a strong bond with each child. I envied Peter his ability to take the kids on worldwide adventures. I took the kids on more low-key vacations to the Washington rainforest and to Montana because big vacations were not my thing—nor were they in my budget. I needed to make my mark some other way.

Leigh is a hard-core animal lover. Her first best friends were our cocker spaniels, who patiently allowed her to dress them in costumes. I have many pictures of Leigh with her "puppies" wrapped in pink boas, or sporting party hats or reindeer antlers. The cockers seemed not to mind—unlike Romeo, our cat. He'd wriggle free from Leigh's suffocating hugs and stride off to roam the neighborhood. When one of our cockers died young from cancer, Leigh bonded even more tightly with the other. She played for hours with Sofie at my house, often disappearing into an imaginary dog world in which she ran around on all fours faster than I could run on two. Peter bought her two cats—and other little critters—that, mercifully, stayed at his house. Leigh made many friends in our neighborhood and at school, but she simply adored her pets and always made time for them.

When Leigh developed a fascination with horses, I seized upon the opportunity to share and to shine. Starting when she was five, Leigh wanted horseback riding lessons, so I helped her learn to ride and care for horses. As she progressed from stable horses to a leased Arabian, I told her stories about Sytan and the wonderful times we'd had galloping around Mercer Island years before, when it was covered with forests and trails. We pored over Arabian magazines and read horse stories. Leigh loved to hear how Sytan would not let anyone but me ride him. As she rode along a short trail near a rental barn, I walked alongside and recounted the adventures I'd enjoyed as a child with Sytan, and later with my horse in California.

When Leigh was ten, Sofie was old and ill, and the vet told me that the dog was holding onto life for us. She said it would be a kindness to put Sofie to sleep. Such a decision would be difficult under any circumstances, but this was my children's dog and Leigh's oldest friend. Leigh bounced in from school one afternoon, unaware that I had carried out the sad task. When I took her aside and broke the news, I expected her to cry. But she went upstairs to her room and shut the door. She didn't want to talk about it. I agonized over what I had done and whether I should have told her first. There didn't seem to be a clear answer, as in so many areas of child rearing. Often, you just do your best and hope for the best.

Days later, while nursing a cup of coffee at Starbucks and feeling bad about Sofie, my eyes fell upon an abandoned newspaper. I picked it up and opened the classifieds. There was only one ad for a horse—an Arabian. Knowing it was bad to try to replace a beloved pet too soon, I paused—then told myself it couldn't hurt to just make a phone call. So I telephoned the horse's owner, a matter-of-fact woman named Lorraine. She told me she was selling one of her five horses because he was burned out on the show ring. Lorraine explained that this horse, named Sydewinder, was an exceptionally pretty horse who had been a Western Pleasure champion for years, but was high strung and fearful. Lorraine said Sydewinder had become too much for her to handle. She rode exclusively in shows, but Sydewinder could no longer take the pressure to perform. I was intrigued and, against my better judgment, made arrangements to look at the horse that very day.

I met up with Lorraine, a lovely woman from a prominent Seattle family, at a gas station, where she showed me Sydewinder's impressive pedigree and show record. I then followed her to the edge of Taylor Mountain, where Lorraine was boarding the horse at a small farm. Sydewinder was a dark bay Arabian with huge, expressive eyes, a perfect star and elegant conformation. As Lorraine watched, I ran my hand along his neck and back and legs. He stood obediently, but flinched and trembled. He watched my movements with white-ringed eyes.

"Is he always this nervous?" I asked Lorraine.

"He frightens easily," she said.

"Will he misbehave when I ride him?"

"He isn't mean, but he'll spin if something scares him."

"It sounds as though his name suits him," I said.

"It does." Lorraine nodded. "He is very quick on his feet."

I rode Sydewinder in an enclosed arena, and he behaved more like a gentleman than Sytan had for my father. Sydewinder's years of professional training shone, and he did precisely what I asked, responding to the slightest touch. In truth, he was more skilled than I. I had never ridden such a finely trained animal. Lorraine and the barn owner, Karen, watched me ride.

"He's being so good for you," Lorraine said.

"You have gentle hands," said Karen.

I had a good feeling about Sydewinder, but told myself to slow down. We had just lost Leigh's dog, her best friend; and here I was practically the next day looking at a burned-out show horse. The barn owner, Karen, had owned and bred Arabians for thirty years, and had shown horses with her daughter. "This horse has a great heart," she said. "He just can't take the pressure of the show ring anymore."

"Sydewinder is nervous," Lorraine said. "I won't mislead you about that. But he deserves to be loved. Why don't you see how your daughter gets along with him?"

Taking a broken-hearted ten-year-old girl to see a horse with no intention of buying it would be cruel. I brought the subject up casually because Leigh was sad and withdrawn over Sofie. She sat silently in the back seat during the hour-long trip to the barn. I hummed along to a CD. When we arrived, Sydewinder was brushed, groomed and clipped. I rode him while Leigh stood silently, looking reticent when I asked if she wanted to try him.

"Okay," she said simply. Sydewinder behaved perfectly, carefully listening to his little rider. When Leigh dismounted, she handed me the reins, still silent.

"I'll call you later," I told Lorraine when we left the barn. I had no idea whether Leigh had liked the horse or not. If she were not up for a special challenge with a special horse, I didn't want to push her. I left Leigh to her own thoughts and decided I'd dodged a bullet. I'd been pretty impulsive to take her in the first place.

When Leigh returned home from school the next day, she smiled and handed me a piece of paper. She'd drawn Sydewinder, precisely capturing his coloring and all his markings. Beneath the drawing, she'd written, "I love him."

❧❦❧

"Peter," I said when he answered his office phone. "You know how much Leigh loves horses, right?"

"Yes," he said. Of course he knew. He had been splitting the cost of horseback riding lessons for five years, not to mention taping Leigh's drawings of horses and unicorns all over his kitchen walls.

"Well, I happened to find this gorgeous Arabian, and I happened to show him to Leigh, and she and I both happened to fall in love with him."

"Umm hmm."

"If we are ever going to buy her a horse, this would be a really good time, because she's ten and would have plenty of time to ride before growing up."

"Are you saying you want to *buy* this horse for Leigh?"

"Yes."

"Do you think you should look at other horses?"

"No, we both love this one."

"Is this a good horse for a little girl?"

"Ah, well, actually, he's a high-strung, burned-out show horse. But he is gorgeous and you can just feel his beautiful soul. This is an extraordinary chance for Leigh to heal a horse's broken heart."

Silence. "I don't want her to get hurt." More silence. "I need to rely on your judgment." Even more silence. "But if you think it's a good idea, I'll go along with it."

❧❧

So just like that, I bought this high-strung, wounded soul for my daughter, and we all began a new journey together. "What a stunning creature he is," I said to Karen one day, marveling that we owned him.

"What a beautiful rider Leigh is," Karen said. "Are you sure you don't want to show him?" she called out to Leigh.

"I'm sure," Leigh answered. "He never has to go into the show ring again."

"We want to take him out on the trails," I said.

"You'll need to work up to it," Karen said. "He's never been ridden beyond a barn or a ring. The first time I took him into a pasture and asked him to step in a mud puddle, he looked at me like I'd lost my mind. But he'll try to do what you ask of him."

Progress with Sydewinder was slow, and I lay awake at night wondering if I'd made a huge mistake. Leigh was madly in love with this horse, although I often doubted he would ever be able to handle a trail. But one morning I woke up with perfect clarity. "I know what I can do," I thought, sitting up in bed. "I can buy another horse. If we have two horses, Leigh and I can ride together on that beautiful mountain near the stable. Forget that I am afraid of big, dark woods! I'll buy a calmer horse that Sydewinder can follow. And we'll get a dog—a big dog to protect us on the trail." This seemed the obvious solution. In the meantime, I needed a horse trailer, which meant that I would need to learn how to pull one.

I called Peter. "Hi."

"Hi. How are things going with Sydewinder?" Peter had already been out to see him and enjoyed seeing Leigh's enthusiasm with her horse. (He, along with Ben, had even helped Karen dig holes for some fence posts, while Leigh and I drank colas and watched. With his first swing of the pick, Ben had hit an underground water line, causing an Old Faithful-like geyser.)

"Great. Things are going great," I said. "Leigh and I are ready to try some trails. But we need a horse trailer to get there. I'm kind of thinking about buying another horse so I can ride with Leigh." I had already gotten a Labrador puppy, Dolly, and was well underway in my search for another horse. "Will you split the cost of a horse trailer with me?"

"Okaaay," Peter said, drawing out the word. "But how will you pull the trailer?"

"Well, I was thinking I could trade cars with *you* when I need to pull the trailer, because your SUV is powerful enough to pull it."

"Fine," Peter said. He hung up without saying goodbye.

By June, I had purchased another Arabian named Salute (and taken a law job downtown to fund all of this). I believed Salute to be calmer than Sydewinder, but he was, in fact, known in the show circuit as "hot"—i.e., a handful. I didn't discover this until after I had purchased him. "I could have told you Salute was hot," Lorraine said in a slightly scolding tone. "You should have asked me." (Lorraine and I liked each other and kept in touch.) She told me that people in the show world could not believe that Sydewinder and Salute—of all horses— were being groomed as trail horses.

It was really no trouble getting Leigh and the horses—and Dolly, the Labrador—to Taylor Mountain and onto the trails. All I had to do was borrow Peter's car, drive Leigh and Dolly to the barn, hook up the horse trailer, load Leigh's horse, load my horse, drive to the trailhead, unload Leigh's horse, unload my horse, tell Dolly to stop barking, saddle my horse, saddle Leigh's horse (whereupon Leigh would spring from the trailer shouting, "I *love* the horse life!"), hoist Leigh onto her horse, free the barking puppy from the car, herd everyone across the road, mount my side-stepping, pawing horse, remember something I forgot, dismount and fetch it, remount my side-stepping, pawing horse, and set off into the forest.

But it was totally worth it. I'll never forget those stunning mountain rides, my long talks with my growing daughter, or the picnics we devoured when we returned, exhausted, to our waiting truck. I would smile to myself, thinking, "These times are mine." As a divorced mom, I felt a constant undercurrent of longing for my children when they were away with Peter, and it was often hard not to envy them having all kinds of fun doing things without me. This, no doubt, explains in part why sharing the "horse life" with Leigh was so important to me, and why I would find myself thinking after a magical ride through the forest with my daughter, "No one else can take these special moments from me."

On one gusty fall day, Leigh and I rode far into the woods. She had been hankering to have her first full-out gallop on Sydewinder, and I thought they were ready. We found a good spot along an old logging road with good footing, and I told Leigh to retrace our steps all the way down to a marsh we often passed, and then gallop Sydewinder back to me and Salute. She eagerly headed off, and Salute snorted and pawed the air while we waited. Sydewinder came streaking up that dirt road, but he settled down beautifully when he reached us. His eyes were filled with joy and wonder, and he was lathered from exertion rather than fear. Leigh and I whooped to celebrate her first real gallop, and she said she couldn't wait to do it again. She had her opportunity, because—of all things—a young black bear fell out of a nearby tree, cracking branches and scaring us witless. We galloped Sydewinder and Salute neck and neck to safety. Our faithful dog Dolly raced along behind.

❡41

When Leigh was eleven, I moved across town to a property where we could keep our horses at home. The property adjoins an equestrian park where Leigh and Sydewinder became known for their wild gallops. Moving away from the community where Peter and I had been jointly raising kids was not a minor undertaking, but it was Leigh's time to come first. That meant surrounding ourselves with the horse life, and Peter supported our move, despite the distance between our two homes. Leigh and I continued to trailer our horses far and wide.

"I feel so lucky that we both love riding, Mom," Leigh said one day, as we rode alongside the Cedar River, which was teeming with bright red salmon. "I want you to know that I know how lucky I am."

"I will treasure these days when I'm sitting in my rocking chair," I said. "I am the luckiest mom alive."

That Thanksgiving, Leigh's school class wrote letters to their parents telling them how they felt thankful. This is what Leigh wrote:

Dear mom and dad,

I am so thankful for you! You are the best parents ever! You know that my dream was to have animals and you were the ones who made that come true. Milana, Midnight, Dolly, Sydewinder and Salute. You got me all those animals! For Mommy, you bought a beautiful house that we could have our horses on. That had been my dream for a long time. For daddy, you made your whole house a kid house, all for us! I am very thankful for that! Also, thank you for naming me such a cool name and making such a good family. Thank you for buying me cool stuff, paying for my school, getting my animals and much more. Also you make me know you love me because even when you two divorced you just moved around the corner. You guys still like each other and respect each other. But the most thing I am thankful for is YOU! I love you! HAPPY THANKSGIVING!

Your daughter,

Leigh

❧❧

"So you're going to teach Leigh about sex, right?" Peter asked. He'd taken the lead on teaching the boys the facts of life, although with the Internet and goodness knows what other sources are available out there, we never did know how timely he'd been.

"Yes, yes," I assured him. "I will."

We'd sent Leigh to an all-girls Catholic school for middle school. She headed off each day in her green plaid skirt, pony tail swinging behind her. When she was in fifth grade, one of the neighborhood moms told me about an upcoming class to be held at a hospital in Seattle. For two Monday evenings in a row, an educator would explain human sexuality to girls who were accompanied by their moms or other significant females. Several of Leigh's friends were going, and I said we'd be happy to go along, too.

The first Monday evening, we showed up along with about 250 other girls and women. As we filed through the door, each girl was handed a white card on which to write questions, which would be provided to the instructor and answered at the end of the session. The first session focused on girls' and boys' different bodies, menstruation, growing up, and the like. There was a bit of giggling and tittering here and there, but it was pretty straightforward overall. The instructor did a good job of explaining the basics. "So what did you think?" I asked as we got in the car to drive home. "Did you learn anything?"

"Not too much," she said.

"Do you want to ask me any questions?"

"Not really."

"Okay, well if you think of any, I'd be happy to talk with you."

"Okay."

The next Monday evening was devoted to human sexuality. The same crowd showed up. As before, the girls were handed white index cards as we filed into the auditorium so they could pass questions to the instructor during the break. This session was a bit odd at times. For example, at one point the instructor stated flatly, "Boys masturbate." A silence fell over the auditorium and I, for one, waited for her to say, "And girls do, too." But she didn't, and I felt she had left an important misimpression.

"Note to self," I thought. "I'm going to have to follow up on that in the car." The instructor completed her presentation and then started reading from the cards that had been gathered during the break. She read out loud from one of them: "Does a person have to be a boy or a girl or can they be both?" With no hesitation, the instructor answered, "A person must be either a boy or a girl. They can't be both."

"Another note to self," I thought. "I need to address that in the car, too."

After the conclusion of the meeting, Leigh and I walked out to the parking lot holding hands. Her pony tail bounced behind her. "Well," I said. "I thought that was pretty good. What did you think?"

"It was fine," she said.

"Umm, there are a couple things I want to clarify," I said as we walked along. "First, the instructor said a person has to be either a boy or a girl. Actually, a person can be born with both male *and* female parts. A person born with both is called a hermaphrodite. Usually they choose the gender that feels most comfortable when they are older."

"Yeah," she said. "I know. That's why I asked."

Needless to say, Leigh already knew about the other subject as well.

❡42

The years fly by faster as we age. Now we have Facebook and other forms of social media, and people chronicle their lives on a daily basis for their friends. But when the kids were growing, I had to use other means to touch bases (at least annually) with friends from California. I liked to send out Christmas letters when I could find the time, and I would shanghai the kids to write a paragraph about their lives. They would sit down and capture something for me, like this:

> *After graduating from Fettes College in Edinburgh I am now beginning my first year at Trinity College Dublin where I am studying English Literature and Film Studies. Thus far my experience in Ireland has been highly enjoyable, both socially and intellectually. Being an American in Europe can be challenging, but at the same time exciting, allowing me to more fully appreciate where I come from. On a basic level life right now is just plain good. What has been referred to as my "work" really consists of reading great*

novels and watching fine films. I supplement this with the music of Brian Wilson and voila: the finer things in life. With a healthy family and a good set of friends there is not much more to ask for. Peace, perhaps? I hope this finds you well and succeeding in all of your various endeavors. Have a happy holidays and always be sure to SMiLE! Peter

Hello everybody. I hope you are all enjoying your holiday. I am busy playing basketball on the Newport Varsity team. We will be heading to San Diego for a holiday tournament soon and that should be a lot of fun. On the whole, things are going well, as I am moving along in my senior year at Newport and trying to finish all my college applications. At this point, I have completed applications to the following universities: University of Washington, University of Texas in Austin, Chapman University in Orange County, Fordham University in New York and Western Washington University in Bellingham. Anyway, there may be a few more applications to come. I hope all is well and I am sure I will see all of you soon. Ben

I have been riding my horse, Sydewinder, almost every day now. My horse is the cutest horse that ever lived on the planet. My mom got a new horse named Shaq. He is really sweet and cute. Shaq is chestnut and has two white feet. We hope he will be a good trail horse. I go to Forest Ridge right now and I am *in 6th grade. I love my teacher. She is so cool. She is engaged right now and I am really happy for her. I have been working with my dog lately on her tricks and agility because I hope to take her to Pet Star and win $25,000. I know I dream big but hey, it could happen. I hope you have a very great holiday season!*

~Leigh

❧43

When I was fourteen, my dad drove Alice from Seattle to Boulder, Colorado, where she was going to college. Linde and I went along, too. That was a great trip, and my father was on his best behavior. Dad read out loud to us in the car, and we filled many hours with conversation, but I spent a great deal of time lost in my own thoughts in the back seat of the car. As we passed through the gorgeous Montana countryside, I gazed out the window at the rolling fields and high-peaked mountains and had an unusual thought. "The love of my life will be a Montana man." I suddenly pictured myself as a mature woman in an open field, examining a fence with a man and discussing whether it needed to be repaired. The thought stayed with me for years because it was so unusual and powerful. I felt deeply connected and bonded to the man and our children. We were in accord with one another. I felt we belonged together. I knew it was a fantasy, but the image stuck with me over the years. Even as I formed relationships with men in my life, I would sometimes think of my Montana fantasy before dismissing it, once again, as a childish dream.

It's possible I met Jim on that trip when I was fourteen. It was the summer before he left Montana to go to Harvard on a four-year scholarship. "They were just driving by and saw me bucking bales in a field," he explains. "They needed to fill a quota from the countryside, so they chose me." I know differently. My Montana man labored in the fields from an early age—but he also labored every night, burning the midnight oil, seeking knowledge, meaning and truth. Harvard plucked him out of that field, and Ethel Roosevelt Derby, Teddy Roosevelt's daughter, paid for his education and tucked him under her generous wing. But before he left Townsend, Montana, that summer of 1967, he worked at the local gas station as he had done for years, pumping gas, changing tires and keeping the cleanest gas station bathroom in all of Montana. Perhaps he pumped gas for our car as we passed through Townsend. He would have shown me and my sisters his beautiful smile while he cleaned helicopter-size bugs from our windshield.

"Maybe I bought a Nehi grape drink from your gas station cooler and drank it while you filled our tank," I once told Jim. We often talked about times our paths may have crossed when we were younger.

"No," he said. "That can't be true. Because if you had come to my gas station, I would have stolen you from your dad's car right then. And we would have been together for the rest of our lives."

Thirty-five years later, I met Jim in the most unlikely of places: a law firm where neither one of us belonged. I was there to support the horse life. He was there practicing law, having made and lost plenty of money, struggling with the after-effects of unhappy marriages and divorce. He longed to pursue his lifelong passion to write. By the end of our first conversation, we were best friends. Over many lunches, we deepened our friendship. I learned that Jim is from a Montana ranching family. His father was reputed to be one of the last great Montana cowboys. Jim is a writer, deep thinker, free spirit, amusing wit and terrific lawyer. He is my Montana man—mature, strong, steady and kind to me.

Shortly after I left the law firm where Jim and I met, he decided to leave too, and to work with me. I believed I'd won the personal lottery to have my best friend and lawyer extraordinaire join me as a law partner. Not long after we established our firm, Jim told me that he loved me. But I had been through too many failed relationships. I told him then about my childhood fantasy about finding my Montana man, with whom I could have a family and fix fences. I told him how much I wished we had met sooner, but that I believed I had exhausted my opportunities to find happiness. There was no question in my mind that if we had met earlier, we could have been happy together—but I feared we were star-crossed and should not become lovers. "There are mountains of obstacles between us," I said.

"Let's take them one mountain pass at a time," he answered.

I still didn't know what to do. We had just started our new firm. I could not imagine being without him, but I didn't see how we could blend our lives. Finally, I decided to go to my mother for guidance. I didn't want to burden her, but I knew I could count on her for honest and correct advice. She was delighted when I called and asked to come see her. I told her

I needed advice on something important, and that I wanted to talk with her in person.

"Jim has told me he loves me. What should I do? What *can* I do?" I asked my mother when we were sitting alone together in her living room. "I feel as though I've burned all my bridges. I've failed at marriage and other relationships too many times."

"I've never met Jim," my mother said. "But I've noticed that whenever you talk about him your face lights up. I've wondered if you weren't in love with him."

"He's my closest friend—the most wonderful man and a great lawyer. But we have only been friends. And it has always been professional. We never even talked about our personal relationships. I don't know what to think."

"How do you feel about him?" she asked. "It seems to me that is the question you need to ask yourself."

I paused, but only briefly. "I love him," I said. "I love him madly."

"Then tell him. You're great friends and you love each other. And if he's as wonderful as you say, everything will turn out all right."

In our office the next day, behind closed doors, I told him, "Yes, I love you, too. I love you and want to be with you for the rest of my life." Jim wrapped his arms around me and held me close. I felt beautiful and loved, safe and protected for the first time in a very, very long time.

❡44

L eigh clicked with Jim from the moment they met. One Sunday morning I listened to them talking on the couch about horses. Jim told Leigh how his Irish ancestors had introduced thoroughbred racehorses into central Montana and how his family had ranched in Montana for generations. Leigh's eyes were wide. He told her his great-grandmother, whom he'd known as a boy, remembered Indians heading east across their land to meet Custer at the Battle of the Little Bighorn. I was getting ready to go to the store for waffle-makings and asked if they wanted to go along. "If it's all right, we'd like to stay and talk," one (or both) said. I knew we were off to a good start.

Jim began riding horses with us. He took over Salute, who was often a handful for me but behaved beautifully for Jim. I bought a lovely chestnut mare, taking her from the show ring and introducing her to the forests and streams. We ventured much farther into the mountains than I would have dared to take Leigh on my own. Together we rode through high mountain meadows filled with spring flowers, swam in icy mountain lakes and cantered in a loose V-formation, mile after mile.

I followed behind Leigh and Jim, reveling in Leigh's happy smiles, our horses' high spirits, and my own fulfillment in love.

Peter's wife, Ellen, is a cultured person who—left to her own devices—might prefer to spend her weekend evenings in relative peace. Having hoards of loud teenagers eating pizza and traipsing back and forth through her house while blasting rap music might not be her cup of tea. But she has graciously shared her home with all three of my children, especially Leigh and her friends. And Ellen's son, Alexander, just a few years younger than Leigh, has suffered the burden of all these teenage girls with remarkable good grace and cheer. Peter simply loves all of the activity congregating in his house in our old neighborhood. Ellen, like Leigh, is tall and slender with oceans of curls. People sometimes say to her, "Your daughter looks just like you!" That's okay, it really is, because Leigh and I know who her mom is, and Ellen does, too.

❦

Jim loved to read with Leigh and shared reading many of the books she was assigned at school. Once when she was in seventh grade, Leigh walked through the kitchen and saw a book sitting on the countertop. "Whose book is this?" she asked, picking it up.

"That's Jim's," I said. "He bought it today."

"What a coincidence!" she said, putting it down and walking off. "I'm reading the same book at school!"

As Leigh finished high school, she began applying to colleges. Having hoped for years that Peter's and my divorce did not harm our children, I was thrilled when she surprised me and Jim with the following essay she had written to accompany a college application:

My parents divorced when I was two years old. Because it happened when I was so young, I've never known anything different. It never really occurs to me that my life is any different than anyone else's; it's just the way I have grown up. Unlike many of my peers' experiences, my parents' divorce was not the traumatic experience that many families go through. My parents remained friends with each other, so I have been lucky.

Over the years, both my parents remarried. While my mother's marriage ended in divorce, she eventually found someone new, a man who treated her wonderfully and made her feel whole. From the very beginning, Jim never imposed on me. He respected the fact that he wasn't my parent. In fact, he never made me do anything; he treated me like an honored guest. I could tell that I was going to like this guy. There was something comforting about him. I could tell that he wasn't just being nice to me because he had to, but because he really wanted me to feel comfortable with him and know that he wasn't there to take my mom away from me. I really appreciated that.

As time went on and we grew more comfortable with each other, we found that we had a lot in common. When we're interested in a particular topic, we both can talk for hours. We would sit by the fire and have endless discussions. He gained more points from me when he helped me with my homework. He would spend hours reading with me or attempting to figure out my math homework. My mom and I now tease him, calling him our human encyclopedia. Somehow, he is able to retain the most random information possible about everything in the world. He is too modest to admit it, but it's true.

In my entire time knowing and living with Jim, I have never seen him get mad or say a cross word. I don't know how he does it, but that man is the closest thing to perfect I have ever seen. If I complain to him about something, he will find some way to make me feel better instantly. If I tell him a new idea I have, he will rave over how good it is and give me more confidence in myself. I always feel better after I talk to him, in part because I know that he will always be there to make things okay. I know I can count on him no matter what.

Having Jim in my life has shown me a new perspective that has made a big difference in the way I see things. I have a mom, step-mom, dad, step-dad, two brothers, two step-brothers and a step-sister. For a while, it was hard to say how I loved them. As

family? As something else entirely? Thinking of Jim,
I realized that you don't have to be able to label how
someone is important to you. Jim isn't my father,
and I know that he will never replace my relationship
with Dad, but he has another huge part of my heart
that can't be defined. Love is there in every form,
and with Jim in my life, I've discovered that we can
always find it in new places.

A few weeks before Leigh finished high school, Peter and I flew with her to Southern California so she could make her final decision on where to go to school. Once again, Peter and I were traveling together with all our attention focused on just one child.

"You look handsome," I told him as the three of us waited for the plane. His hair is silver and short—no longer the shoulder-length, dark hair he had when we were law students so long ago. He is a successful businessman and a great dad.

"Thank you," he said and smiled. Leigh looked back and forth between us. I could see that our friendship gives her comfort. She deeply loves us both.

Peter and I sat together on the full airplane—Leigh sat under headphones across the aisle. For two uninterrupted hours, Peter and I talked about our three children. We spoke of pride, hopes, concerns—in short, of our mutual love for our grown children.

Peter and I have become close friends in a way I would never have imagined we could before our divorce. He is a fantastic father to our children, and he recently told me, "You are the best mama ever." Wherever I go, I will be with Jim. But I will also hold Peter close in my heart. Yes, divorce with children can be a disaster. But it doesn't have to be. As parents, we can and should choose peace.

❡EPILOGUE

I asked my sons — while emphasizing they should feel *no pressure* — to write a few paragraphs for my epilogue. They have both done so, and their twisted arms are recovering nicely! In between his college finals, job interviews, and DJing at large parties, Ben wrote the following words:

> *I am very fortunate to have parents who prioritized the well being of their children throughout their divorce. Although all divorces will be painful to each family member in their own way, I believe strongly that there is a way to transition positively and maintain a loving and healthy family.*
>
> *Over the years I feel my parents' commitment to us kids has ultimately created a stronger bond between the two of them, and it's been wonderful to be able to celebrate holidays and all sorts of events with the two of them together as friends. The stability they created while working together as parents has been fundamental to my confident and joyous outlook on*

life. I can say with certainty that my parents' divorce has not diminished the love and strength of our family bonds.

Peter Jr., who shares my love of writing and of pondering the human condition—graciously wrote:

Though I come from a divorced family, I do not come from a broken family. This, I believe, is the ultimate distinction that influences the happiness of all involved. Divorced families need not be broken families, though it is a sad truth that all too often they are. That alone makes what my parents managed to build together all the more remarkable. Broken families are defined by a destructive dynamic, one in which the sum serves as a distressing factor, perhaps the distressing factor, in the lives of its parts. Though it is difficult at this stage in my life to come to any definitive conclusions regarding myself, my family and the circumstances in which I grew up (as I imagine to an extent it always will be), I can say with certainty that the above description bears no relation to the people I happily call my own.

"I love you more than life itself." My Mom said this to me quite often growing up. She says it still today. As a child I took it for granted. How could I not? It was just one of those things my mom told me, interwoven into the fabric of the only life I knew. However, as my experience broadens I think am beginning (only beginning, mind you) to understand, to grasp at

the edges, its significance. Far more than simply influencing my emotions—whether or not I'm happy or sad at any given moment—it has made me who I am. Though that in many ways remains a mystery, I know that I am loved. If I never learn anything else, I'll die a happy man. More and more I meet people who've never had anyone tell them they are loved. It breaks my heart because deep down inside I fear they feel that perhaps they don't deserve to be loved. To convince someone in this sorry state of affairs otherwise, to my mind, is to give meaning to this unique experience of being human.

Of course, my mom has done much more than simply tell me she loves me; she's given the words full expression through the life she's lived and the sacrifices she's made. At the same time, I realize that my mother's love is far greater than I am. If I am lucky enough to have children, I too will have to dedicate a lifetime if I am to provide them the life of love she's striven so hard to provide me. She's given me the strength to do this. In this sense, her love is bigger than us both. It is a cliché to say that I can never repay her for all that she's done, but it's true. Even now I realize I could do more. More than that, I should do more. Let me at least begin. Mom, I love you more than life itself . . .

Of all the beautiful sentiments my children have expressed over the years, the one that most fills me with joy and hope for the future is that they, too, look forward to the great good fortune of having children. They believe their parents—even though divorced—provided them with love and peace. Isn't that what matters most, after all?

Yes, I look forward someday to being a grandmother and to watching my children raise their own children with love. I can already picture the moment when Jim and I and Peter and Ellen and all our kids gather around the first grandchild, saying, "*Objectively speaking,* is this not the most beautiful baby in the world?"

❧ACKNOWLEDGMENTS

Thank you to my ex-husband, Peter: Our marriage did not last "till death do us part," but we were married fourteen years and had three beautiful children. Learning to share our children and to cooperate in raising them after our divorce has been my proudest accomplishment. Thank you for sharing this journey, for being a wonderful father, for supporting my publication of this book, and for becoming, and remaining, such a steadfast friend to me.

Thank you to my children, Peter Jr., Ben and Leigh, for filling my life with joy and for giving me such enthusiastic encouragement to share our family's "divorce story."

Thank you to my Mom and Dad who so generously encouraged me to tell this story in hopes that our experience can help others struggling with the challenges of raising children with an ex. Huge thanks also to my three siblings who not only have shared so much of my life but read my manuscript and told me to go for it!

Thank you to my editors, Ceci Miller and Lisa Gordanier, for helping me hone the story to its most essential elements and for providing me with so much wisdom, honesty and insight.

To my husband, Jim, my love and best friend, thank you for your tireless reading and editing of my manuscript and for cheering me on when I wondered whether I could or should share this story in a meaningful way.